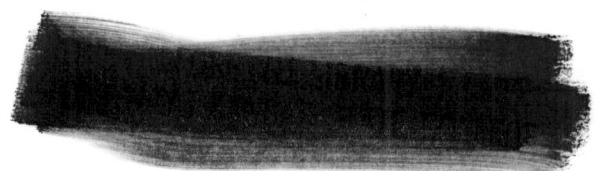

WITHDRAWN

BREEDING BIOLOGY OF THE GRAY GULL, *Larus modestus*

BREEDING BIOLOGY OF THE GRAY GULL, *Larus modestus*

BY

THOMAS R. HOWELL, BRAULIO ARAYA,
and WILLIAM R. MILLIE

UNIVERSITY OF CALIFORNIA PRESS
BERKELEY · LOS ANGELES · LONDON
1974

Advisory Editors: G. A. Bartholomew, J. H. Connell, John Davis,
C. R. Goldman, Cadet Hand, K. S. Norris, O. P. Pearson,
R. H. Rosenblatt, Grover Stephens

University of California Publications in Zoology
Volume 104

Approved for publication December 14, 1973
Issued November 15, 1974

University of California Press
Berkeley and Los Angeles
California

University of California Press, Ltd.
London, England

591.08
C153u
v. 104
1974

ISBN: 0-520-09516-2
Library of Congress Catalog Card Number: 73-620262

© 1974 by the Regents of the University of California
Printed in the United States of America

To the late Dr. Rudolfo A. Philippi B. (1905-1969), distinguished ornithologist and physician, inspiring mentor and companion, who maintained a family tradition of biological research in Chile that extends back through three generations.

CONTENTS

Introduction	1
Acknowledgments	
Description and General Habits	2
Courtship and Mating Behavior on the Coast	3
Behavior in the Desert Nesting Area	7
Size of Colony and Distribution of Nests	13
Clutch Size	14
The Egg	16
Location of Nest by Returning Adults at Night	17
Incubation Behavior	18
Incubation Temperatures	19
Incubation Period	23
The Chick	24
Nestling Care	25
Food	28
Growth of Chicks	30
Thermoregulation	31
Mortality among Young Birds	34
Predation	35
Nocturnal Activity of Adults on the Coast	36
Juveniles on the Coast	37
The Pampa in the Nonbreeding Season	37
Discussion	38
Ethology	38
A behavioral analogy	44
Desert nesting: Advantages and adaptations	45
Taxonomic relationships	48
Plumage color	49
Origin of desert nesting	53
Summary	53
Literature Cited	55

BREEDING BIOLOGY OF THE GRAY GULL, *Larus modestus*

BY

THOMAS R. HOWELL, BRAULIO ARAYA, and WILLIAM R. MILLIE

INTRODUCTION

The Gray Gull, *Larus modestus*, is an abundant bird along most of the Pacific coast of South America. Its main range extends from about 0° to 40° S latitude, from Manta, Ecuador, to Valdivia, Chile. Despite the Gray Gull's abundance, its nest, eggs, and breeding locations were unknown to science at the time of Murphy's (1936) classic work on the oceanic birds of South America. Murphy pointed out that it did not nest on offshore islands or along the coast, and guessed that it might nest in the barren deserts of the interior. Unknown to Murphy, A. W. Johnson had found a nesting colony and collected eggs of this species in the desert of northern Chile in 1919. In 1943, Johnson, J. D. Goodall, and the late R. A. Philippi located another desert colony in Chile and described the nest and eggs (Goodall, Philippi, and Johnson, 1945). Johnson (1967) gives a full account of these events. An interesting coincidence is that Murphy (1936:265) quoted an account by an old resident of the Chilean nitrate desert about "a kind of 'gull', locally called 'Garuma', which nests in such situations. The adults return only at night, bringing fish, and their cries are heard all through the hours of darkness." Murphy was not familiar with the Chilean name for this species and the behavior seemed so un-gull-like that he surmised that the birds must be petrels, but the old resident's tale proves to be substantially correct. Another interesting account comes from the father of Braulio Araya. The senior Araya worked in the nitrate deserts near Los Dones, Antofagasta Province, in 1906, and he recalls that young gulls were taken from a nesting colony, raised on food scraps, and then eaten.

Among ornithologists, virtually all that was known of the Gray Gull until 1968 is included in the references above and in Moynihan's (1962) study of its hostile and sexual behavior as observed on the coast. Moynihan did not visit a nesting colony of this species, but his descriptions of postures and vocalizations are very thorough. Since these authors are cited many times in the following sections, we do not repeat the date of publication after their names each time. From this point on, unless otherwise mentioned, citation of Murphy, Moynihan, or Johnson[1] refers to their publications of 1936, 1962, and 1967, respectively.

The nesting colony discovered by Goodall, Philippi, and Johnson in 1943 was visited by them only briefly and early in the breeding cycle; they could

---

[1]Johnson (1967) is an updated revision in English of volume II of *Las Aves de Chile* (1951) by Goodall, Johnson, and Philippi, in which the authors' names were listed in alphabetical order. The earlier version will be more familiar to Spanish-speaking readers, but the 1967 edition includes newer information and is thus cited here.

provide few details of nesting behavior and nothing, of course, about hatchlings and their care and development. For the most part, the behavioral or physiological adaptations that would enable a seabird to reproduce successfully in the most barren desert on earth remained unknown. To study these adaptations, Howell visited coastal areas and an interior nesting colony of Gray Gulls in Chile in November and December 1968, and all three of the present authors visited the same areas in January and February 1970. During these visits we studied the birds' activities both on the coast and in the nesting colony. Exact dates and localities are given in later sections.

ACKNOWLEDGMENTS

We gratefully acknowledge the advice and assistance of the many persons and the organizations that made this study possible. Financial support included a grant to Howell from the National Geographic Society, and the Universidad de Chile–University of California Cooperative Program provided some funding, the use of a field vehicle, and all manner of helpful assistance from the personnel of the Santiago office. The personal interest of Mr. Leland G. Means of the Compañía Anglo-Lautaro secured for us the generous cooperation of the company's personnel at Pedro de Valdivia and María Elena. We are especially grateful to Oreste Hernandez, Técnico Minero at María Elena, who guided us to the gull nesting colony and aided in many other ways. George Moffett, Jr., visited the colony shortly after Howell's 1968 visit, published a short account (Moffett, 1969), and generously provided copies of some photographs. S. E. Chapman of Southampton, England, visited the colony in 1971, also published a brief account (Chapman, 1973), and graciously deferred plans for further publication until this long report was completed. Adrian Brown and his family made available information on coastal activities of the gulls and made possible some of our coastal observations. J. D. Goodall was particularly helpful to the senior author on all his visits to Chile. Special acknowledgment is due A. W. Johnson, the first ornithologist to locate the nesting area of the Gray Gull, eminent authority on the birds of Chile, and a continuous source of encouragement and assistance in the course of our research.

DESCRIPTION AND GENERAL HABITS

The Gray Gull is of moderate size, and the general appearance of the bird is shown in the accompanying plates. Murphy gives detailed plumage descriptions and measurements. *Larus modestus* resembles *L. heermanni* of the Pacific coast of Mexico and North America but has a black bill with a pinkish orange lining instead of a red bill as does *heermanni*. Adults of both these species have a nonbreeding plumage with a dark head instead of white. The Lava Gull, *L. fuliginosus,* of the Galápagos Islands is also largely gray, and these three species may or may not be a closely related group (see Discussion).

Along the coast, Gray Gulls inhabit rocky and sandy beaches where they often feed like sandpipers in the wash of the waves (pl. 1), as described by

Murphy and Johnson. By probing in the sand they capture burrowing crabs, *Emerita analoga* (Murphy, Johnson, this study), which are abundant and probably important in the gulls' diet. Gray Gulls also scavenge around harbors and offshore fishing boats, and they may join other seabirds over great schools of fish when these come close to shore. We have seen large fish disgorged by Gray Gulls in courtship and in feeding young but do not know how these were obtained.

Gray Gulls occur along the coast throughout the year, including the breeding season. Murphy mentions that specimens collected in October, 1919, at the Chincha Islands, Peru, "were clearly at the verge of their season of reproduction." Gray Gulls disappeared from the islands about the middle of November, but remained numerous on the continental beaches in December. Johnson and Moynihan describe the evening departure and early morning return of Gray Gulls from the Chilean coast from November to January. All the evidence indicates that the breeding season begins around November and is confined to the austral summer. There are no certain records of Gray Gulls from the interior at other times of year.

The only known breeding sites are those listed by Johnson; all are in the deserts of northern Chile. These few colonies could hardly produce such a large population, and other sites will probably be found elsewhere in Chile and in similar areas in Peru. The nesting of this species is almost certainly confined to the barren desert region as the birds are too conspicuous to have been overlooked if they bred in other habitats.

COURTSHIP AND MATING BEHAVIOR ON THE COAST

The only published observations giving details of hostile and sexual displays of the Gray Gull are those of Moynihan, who studied these birds on the coast in the vicinity of Antofagasta, Chile, from 24 November to 6 December 1955. Howell visited the same area from 28-30 November, 6-9 and 15-16 December 1968, and all of us made observations on 19-20 and 27-28 January 1970. In that city, the prominent Hotel Antofagasta faces a small bay that includes an expanse of flat rocks dissected by narrow channels. Except when covered by high tides, the rocks are frequented by a large number of Gray Gulls as well as by Neotropic Cormorants *(Phalacrocorax olivaceus)*, Brown Pelicans *(Pelecanus occidentalis)*, Kelp Gulls *(Larus dominicanus)*, and wintering flocks of Franklin Gulls *(Larus pipixcan)* and Elegant Terns *(Sterna elegans)*; when high tide covers the rocks the birds take to the water or seek other locations. This small bay is an especially favorable place to observe Gray Gulls as they are numerous there and relatively unwary. Other coastal localities where we studied gulls include La Chimba, 10 km north of Antofagasta, where there is a rocky amphitheater-like formation above high-tide level, and Hornito, 84 km north of Antofagasta, where there is sandy beach with some rock outcrops and islets.

We follow Moynihan's terminology for the postures and vocalizations of the Gray Gull; it is largely derived from that of Tinbergen and is in use by other students of gull behavior. Capital letters are used to indicate these terms and many of the displays are figured in the plates. We were able to recognize most of the behavior patterns and calls from Moynihan's descriptions and drawings but found the Long Call different from his transcription. In our experience, the Long Call was usually a series of six, not four, rapid short notes, followed by a single long-drawn note. Numerous tape recordings by us confirm this as the typical Long Call pattern; Dr. Moynihan has heard the recordings and concurs.

We found, as Moynihan did, that along the coast the Gray Gulls carry on aggressive behavior, courtship, and copulation—indeed, almost the full spectrum of social behavior of adults. The following account summarizes the courtship and mating behavior of Gray Gulls as observed by us on the coast in the vicinity of Antofagasta. In general, the behavior is very similar to that described by Tinbergen (1953, 1959) for the Herring Gull *(Larus argentatus)* and other *Larus* species.

Antofagasta is virtually at the Tropic of Capricorn, and during early December the period from sunrise to sunset is about 14 hours. At this season about 95 percent of the Gray Gulls along the coast are in definitive adult plumage. Almost all leave the coast within one or two hours after sunset, often in large wheeling flocks but also individually and in small groups that move locally north or south before heading inland. We did not see the birds heading directly for the interior, and they probably do not do so until after dark. We found no gulls at night in the same rocky areas that teemed with them during the day. Shortly before sunrise, Gray Gulls begin to arrive at the rocks at Antofagasta from up or down the coast; we did not see them coming in from the desert to the east. At first they are spaced out on the rocks about 6 to 8 body-lengths (2.4 to 3.2 m) apart, but as more birds arrive the spacing diminishes, and by about an hour after sunrise gulls are no more than 2 or 3 lengths apart (0.8 to 2.4 m). On 7 December 1968, at low tide, Howell recorded about 26 pairs in a rocky area 26 x 14 m; this approximates an average of one pair per 14 m^2, but the birds were not uniformly spaced and the total number present in the area was several hundred. There is a high turnover, with birds continuously leaving for and arriving from the sea. Without marked birds we could not tell if the same individuals returned to a particular site during the same or successive days, but one bird with a distinctive plumage marking occupied the same general area on two consecutive days.

The gulls did not seem to attempt vigorous defense of a territory against all intruders but usually reacted aggressively only if another bird came within reach or approached during courtship feeding or precopulatory behavior. Aggressive behavior may be expressed by an Aggressive Upright, an advance in Low Oblique Posture, or a lunge with wings raised and bill gaped; either sex may show such behavior. On the coastal territories actual fights are very rare.

In a typical pattern of mating behavior, two birds stand beside each other or one flies in and alights next to the other. One assumes a Hunched Posture, with the head lowered even with or perhaps below the level of the back, but with the bill parallel to the substrate. The remiges are slightly drooped and spread, accentuating the conspicuousness of the white terminal band of the secondaries. The Hunched bird then paces back and forth before the other one, and the posture may change to the Low Oblique in which the neck is somewhat extended and arched. The soliciting bird is usually a female and she may give the Mew Call, which in *L. modestus* is a prolonged moan rather than a "mew" sound. The male may also give the same call. The male of a pair often appears to have a slightly Crested Head-set, and the female an Egg-shaped Head-set. Then both birds begin Head-tossing, throwing the head quickly upward so that the bill points vertically or even "overshoots" as much as 20° beyond straight up, and then returns to approximately horizontal. Head-tossing may be given in any posture from Hunched to Low Oblique, Oblique, or Upright. The bill is gaped during Head-tossing, showing the pinkish-orange lining of the otherwise all-black bill, and a single soft plaintive call note (Kioo) is given. The birds do not always face each other during Head-tossing, and may be oriented at different angles and even parallel but head-to-tail. When they face each other, there may be Facing Away (Head-flagging) by one or both birds between Head-tosses. The female of the pair repeatedly nibbles at the male's bill, and he often responds by arching his neck, lowering his head (Low Oblique Posture), and disgorging a mass of fish. This may be seized and swallowed by the female as it appears, or it may drop on the rock and be eaten there. Sometimes the male allows only part to fall to the female, sometimes he pulls some of it back, or he may occasionally recover and reswallow all of it.

After the fish-disgorging and eating, one or both birds may go and dip their bills in the nearest available water, shaking the head from side to side a few times. There are no swallowing movements or other indications of drinking. Similar behavior was described by Moynihan (1955a) in swimming pairs of *Larus ridibundus*. Moynihan suggests that this is rinsing of the bill after mouthing disgorged fish, but the Gray Gull sometimes performs bill-washing without any prior disgorging or eating and the gesture may have some other significance. On one occasion a female twice carried a piece of disgorged food into the water and shook it vigorously but lost it in the process the second time.

Whether or not Bill-washing occurs, there is more Head-tossing. The male may then pace in partly Hunched or Low Oblique Posture around the female, often attempting to bring his bill over her nape or back and then to mount. The female often turns as the male attempts this, so that both birds circle and there may be more Head-tossing and Facing Away. If the female stands still and crouches, the male mounts her with a hop and wing-flap and places his feet far anteriorly on her scapulars and on the wings near the carpal joints. Settling on his tarsi, he then raises his wings to about 45-60° above horizontal and may flap them slightly in keeping balance. He lowers his tail on one or the other side of hers and waggles it back and forth. The female may raise her rectrices about 15-20° as the male mounts, or do so only after his tail feathers push against hers. The male's head points obliquely down, and the female may raise hers—even give a Head-toss—and the birds may grasp bills. When he first mounts, the male usually takes up to 30 seconds of standing and balancing before lowering his tail, and then makes several attempts at cloacal contact during the next 60 to 90 seconds. During attempts at cloacal contact, the male opens his beak slightly and gives a repetitive monotone Copulation Call; it is often audible only at close range and is perhaps not always given. If the female remains receptive, the male usually dismounts or falls off between 90 to 180 seconds after initially mounting. If the female is not fully receptive, she takes a few steps forward and this usually dislodges the male.

Moynihan provides a thorough description of pair-formation, early pairing reactions, and later pairing as observed at Antofagasta, and our observations at the same place are in accord. Of particular interest are the semiterritorial communal gatherings on the rocks. As the rocks are mostly covered at high tide and as the birds leave the coast every night and return the next morning from a great distance, there is little possibility of strongly defined and relatively permanent territories. In any case, mating activity goes on at high intensity from dawn to dusk, and although there is often low-intensity aggression between neighboring birds, courting and copulating pairs may be only 1 m apart without conflict.

Moynihan treated the later pairing and mating behavior in the Gray Gull only briefly as it is generally similar to that of many other larids. We give here a fuller account as we noted some details not previously recorded.

At Antofagasta, the regurgitation-feeding phase was often interrupted by an aggressive Kelp Gull or Band-tailed Gull *(L. belcheri)* that rushed up and tried to seize the disgorged fish. Copulations were often disrupted by a third Gray Gull attempting to mount the already mounted male. The third bird, presumably another male, frequently succeeded in mounting and often proved surprisingly difficult to dislodge. These disturbances point up the reproductive advantages of maintaining a territory that excludes intruders.

Occasionally, we were able to keep track of inividual birds during their activities on the rocks. On the morning of 7 December 1968, Howell saw both members of a pair, together and individually, using Aggressive Upright Postures to drive away other Gray Gulls that approached this pair before and after courtship feeding behavior.

Sometimes a male attempts to solicit interest of a female by assuming a Hunched and then a Low Oblique Posture, pacing back and forth before her, and disgorging a fish without any soliciting activity by the female. Howell watched such behavior on 7 December 1968; the male brought up a small fish that he held in his bill, and when the female showed no interest, he reswallowed it.

On the same day, an individually recognizable male attempted to court successively two different birds that were only 2 m apart. This male chased away two other gulls, but neither female responded to his back-and-forth pacing and he flew out to sea.

Once, a female successfully solicited regurgitation-feeding from a male while both were swimming beside the rocks.

An edited paraphrase from Howell's tape-recorded notes of 7 December 1968 touches on many aspects of coastal behavior:

A pair starts courting on the rocks, but the male appears uneasy—perhaps because of a Kelp Gull and another Gray Gull close by. He walks back and forth in Low Oblique Posture, and then the female persistently solicits from him in Hunched Posture, bringing her bill close to his as though expecting a disgorged fish. He moves off in a Low Oblique run and then flies to another rock 15 m away, and then to a rock another 10 m beyond. The female follows him, actively soliciting and aggressively displaces another Gray Gull from an adjacent rock. The pair is now within 2 or 3 m of four other gulls, and the male flies another 20 m to a different rock, followed by the female. He gives a Long Call and displaces another bird. The female resumes soliciting, and he assumes a more Hunched Posture but then flies another 2 m farther on. The pair has now moved over 50 m from their original location, and passed through the "territories" of at least four other pairs. The pair begins circling and Head-tossing; the female nibbles at his bill, and he at last disgorges a fish, which she eats. Both birds Head-toss, and the male briefly attempts to mount. Then he paces back and forth obliquely in front of her; both Head-toss, and the male mounts. The female continues Head-tossing, and the male briefly grasps her upturned bill with his. One minute after mounting he attempts cloacal contact; five other attempts follow at approximately 10-second intervals. About two minutes after the initial mounting, another Gray Gull flies over and seems about to alight on the male's back. He leaps into the air at this threat, and that concludes the mating.

Occasionally, one or both birds of two that behaved aggressively toward each other would turn away and grasp a projecting piece of rock with the bill and tug at it. This appears to be the homologue of Grass-pulling or Pecking-into-the-ground in other species of *Larus,* but grass is of course lacking over most of the land frequented by the Gray Gull.

Although most of the postures and vocalizations of the Gray Gull are similar to those of many better-known species, some are distinctly different. As mentioned, the Long Call usually consists of six short notes followed by a long-drawn note. Occasionally, one or two additional short notes are included before the last one. When giving the Long Call, the Gray Gull does not first lower its head or point its bill down, but starts the call from a horizontal position of the head (Oblique Posture, pl. 3), raising it to vertical as the call is given (pls. 16, 17). The Mew Call, usually given from a Low Oblique position, does not sound like its name but is a weird moan reminiscent of some calls of shearwaters *(Puffinus* sp.*).* We found the Landing Call of Moynihan difficult to distinguish from the Long Call Note, and noted that landings were frequently silent.

BEHAVIOR IN THE DESERT NESTING AREA

On 30 November 1968, Howell began a study of a nesting colony in the Pampa del Miraje, east of Cerro Colupo, at 18 km WNW of Pedro de Valdivia, Antofagasta, at an elevation of about 1,800 m and about 30 km from the coast. This is the same location visited by Goodall, Johnson, and Philippi in 1943, and was reached with the aid of Oreste Hernandez, Técnico Minero of the Companía Anglo-Lautaro and a highly knowledgeable explorer of that region.

The desert of northern Chile is probably the driest on earth, for rain has never been recorded in some areas and only at intervals of many years in others. If rain has fallen within historic times in the Pampa del Miraje, there is no biological evidence of it. The soil is totally dry, in some places as powdery as flour and in others sandy, but generally strewn with rocks ranging in size from small pebbles to angular stones that are mostly less than 0.3 m in greatest dimension. There is no trace of vegetation and no permanently resident animal life of any kind. Without even the beginning of a food chain, the only animals to be found are those that can travel long distances from other areas where life can be permanently sustained.

In late 1968 and early 1970, air temperatures ranged from a low of about 2.5° C at night to a high of about 38° at about midday. Surface temperatures in the sun were often higher than 50°, which was the maximum limit of our instruments, and we recorded relative humidities as low as 8 percent. There are sometimes heavy fogs in parts of the region, but we experienced no fog in the gull nesting colony in the Pampa del Miraje during our stays there.

Wind is an important climatic influence in the Pampa del Miraje. The air was usually calm or only slightly windy from the north during mornings and nights, at least from late November through February, but there is invariably a strong and continuous wind that begins within 7 or 8 hours after sunrise and continues at least until sunset. This wind is always from approximately the WSW and presumably comes from the coast through an area of relatively low relief. The afternoon wind blows steadily, always strong and with velocities up to 20 mph; its effect on the nesting gulls is discussed subsequently.

At the times of Howell's first visits, from 30 November to 9 December 1968, gulls were sporadically present during the day but only in small numbers not exceeding about 100. On one day many would be present, showing some territorial and courtship behavior, and on other days during this interval not one could be found. For example, on the afternoon of 30 November there were about 100 birds spaced out through a large area containing fresh nest scrapes, but there was little overt territorial behavior. Howell returned to the same place at sunrise on 2 December, saw 5 gulls only as they flew away toward the coast, and searched a wide area on foot for the next 14 hours, until dark, without finding a single gull. On the afternoon of 3 December gulls were again abundant in the same area. On 4 December Howell returned just before sunrise; a tight flock of about 100 birds wheeled and circled high and low over the colony for the next 2 hours, alighting once for about 20 minutes, then taking wing again and finally disappearing toward the coast. During the rest of the daylight hours, only a group of 12 resting, nonterritorial birds was located and they flew off in the late afternoon.

Although there were many fresh nest scrapes and tracks around them, an exhaustive search revealed no eggs. On 9 December only a single bird was seen at nightfall, but by about one hour after dark some Long Call Notes were heard and within the next hour many hundreds of birds arrived. The valley resounded with the full repertoire of Gray Gull vocalizations, including Long Calls, the Mew Call, Head-toss Notes, and Copulation Calls, showing that territorial and mating behavior was at high intensity. After dawn these activities diminished greatly, and although an estimated 2,000 birds were present, they were relatively inactive and quiet.

Subsequent observations until 15 December showed that gulls were present during the day with greater regularity and in increasing numbers, and that they arrived in large numbers at night. No eggs were found until 11 December, and there were still very few by the time of Howell's departure on 15 December. Thus, most of the 1968 desert observations are of the pre-egg stage.

In the nesting colony during the day in the pre-egg stage, birds were spaced much more widely than in the transient territories on the coast, and mating behavior was less pronounced. Birds by nest scrapes were usually about 5 to 10 meters from their nearest neighbor, and many birds were either unpaired or the mate was absent. Some assembled in Clubs of as many as 200 birds, and occasionally there were silent Panic Flights or Dreads in which up to 100 birds took to the air and formed a dense, fast-moving flock that wheeled and swooped about like a group of sandpipers but without any evident cause for alarm. Tinbergen's suggestion (1953, 1964) that these flights in *L. argentatus* are an expression of fear of the breeding habitat and the possibility of concealed predators does not seem applicable to *L. modestus*, whose breeding habitat is extremely open and virtually lacks terrestrial predators.

The nest scrape is a circular depression in the ground about 200-230 mm in diameter and about 35 mm deep in the center, and each member of a pair may make one or more scrapes. We never saw a bird gather or place any material around the nest although small pebbles, feathers, and parts of desiccated carcasses are readily available. Occasional accumulations of such materials around a nest probably represent windblown debris or the accidental results of scrape excavation. Scrapes may or may not be located beside a rock, and if so they are not usually placed on a particular side. At this latitude and season, the sun is almost directly overhead during the hottest part of the day and the rocks then provide little useful shade; we doubt that there is any adaptive advantage in placing a nest scrape beside one of the innumerable, randomly scattered rocks.

The rocks, however, are important in the adult gulls' thermoregulatory activity. The sandy substrate heats rapidly in the sun and by midmorning the substrate temperatures may exceed 50°C. The rock surfaces are smoother and reflect much more heat than the sandy substrate. By 3 or 4 hours after sunrise, most birds move off the sand and stand on rocks with their feet shaded by their own bodies (pl. 4); the exceptions are those birds that have been sitting on nest scrapes with their feet under them since the cool early morning. On 13 December 1968, from 1115 to 1415, soil exposed to full sun but shaded as the thermistor probe was applied showed a rise in temperature over the three-hour period from 39.4° to more than 50°. Rock surface temperatures at the same time under identical conditions ranged from 38.4° to 41.4° (fig. 1). After many hours in full sun, rock temperatures in early after-

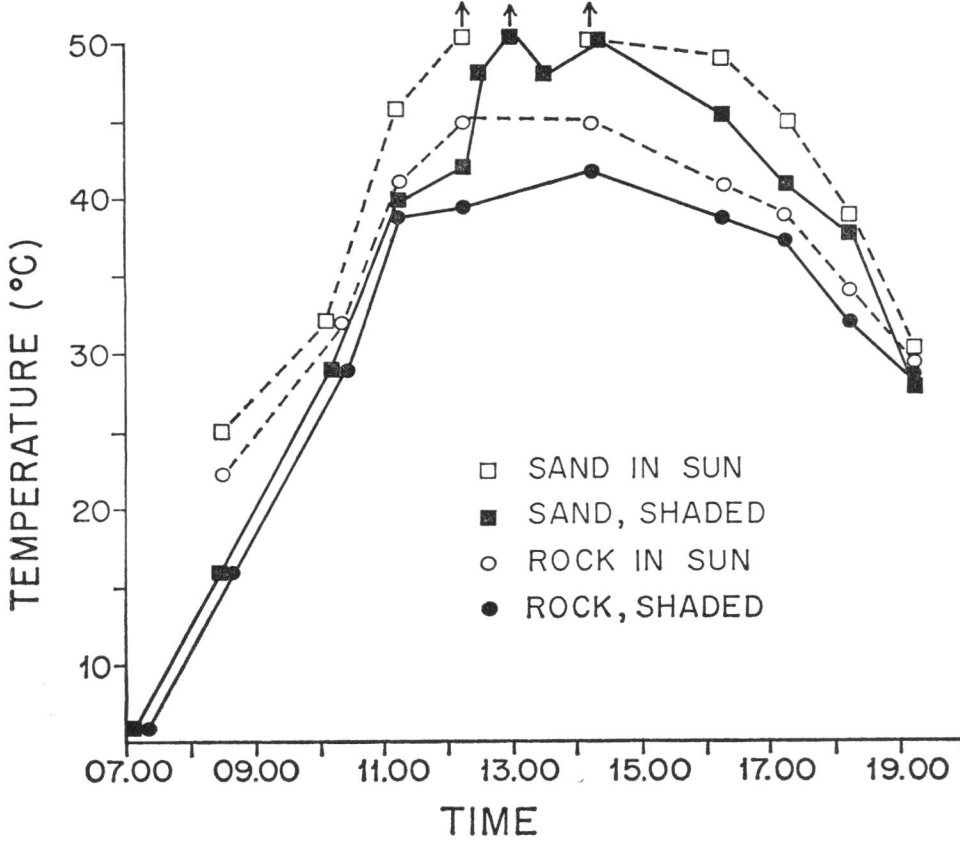

Fig. 1. Substrate temperatures at a Gray Gull nest site on 13 December 1968. Shaded temperatures were obtained by shading the surface as the thermistor probe was applied to it. Symbols with upward-pointing arrows indicate readings above 50°, the upper limit of the instrument. Strong WSW wind began at about 1300 and continued throughout the afternoon.

noon might reach 45°, but they were always much lower (usually less than 40°) in late morning when gulls began to stand on them. This rock-standing allows the birds to minimize heat gain from the sandy substrate without having to take to the air and may also increase heat loss by convective cooling.

Possibly because of the heat stress in the desert during the day, the gulls are far more active there at night in all of their reproductive behavior. Unfortunately and surprisingly, the gulls are extremely wary at night and the beam of a flashlight causes great alarm that quickly spreads through the colony. Our nocturnal observations were made by moonlight from a canvas blind or a stationary vehicle without lights. In the clear desert air, however, the moon is extremely bright and full moonlight provides good visibility at close range. We obtained our best data on pre-egg territorial behavior in the nesting colony on the night of 24-25 January 1970, when we spent the entire night in a part of the colony that included birds incubating eggs and birds still in the pre-egg stage. We distinguished three territories adjacent to one another in which eggs were not yet present. The territory closest to us was continuously patrolled by an extremely active bird that we assumed to be a male. He became especially noticeable about two hours after dark, when the moon rose, and he may have arrived from the coast or may have been stimulated by the arrival of others at that time. In about the center of his territory were two pairs of rocks about 2 m apart; he frequently stood on the rocks and gave Long Calls, and from this central location quickly moved

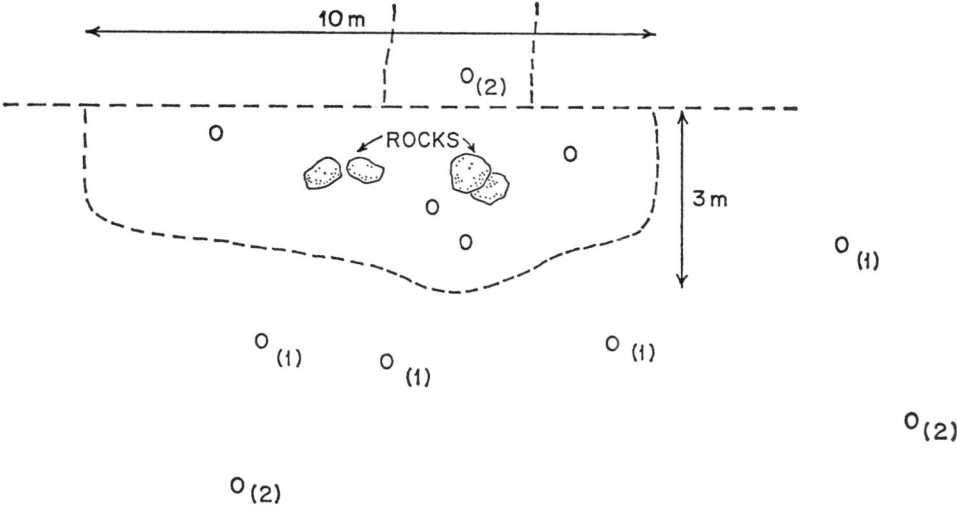

Fig. 2. Territories of Gray Gulls in pre-egg stage observed during night of 24-25 January 1970, enclosed in dashed lines, and adjacent occupied nests. Open circles indicate nest scrapes and numbers in parentheses indicate numbers of eggs present, if any. See text for additional details.

toward any bird that crossed his apparent territorial perimeter. The territory seemed to be roughly rectangular, about 10 m by 3 m at the widest, with the perching rocks central. Territories of two other nonincubating birds and of one with eggs were staggered along one side of the long axis, and those of several incubating birds were on the opposite (fig. 2). We did not see definite conflicts limiting the bird in the long dimension, and possibly he did not attempt to defend an extent more than 5 m in either direction beyond his perching rocks. When a bird appeared to enter his territory, the male might assume an Aggressive Upright Posture or give Long Calls (especially toward flying birds) or run toward the intruder in Low Oblique Posture. Although we could not distinguish individuals with certainty, there seemed to be one presumed female and thus a potential mate that repeatedly entered the area. As the male approached her, he gave moaning Mew Calls, and she commenced Choking (pl. 19) while giving repeated muffled yelping calls. The male often assumed the same posture beside her. This behavior pattern is extremely similar to nest scrape–making, and in these instances scrapes were definitely being formed by rubbing the breast feathers in the sand and pushing posteriorly with the feet. The territory included at least four scrapes and both birds were involved in scrape-making, with each bird working on each of the scrapes at one or another time.

The territorial male continued his vigorous activity well into the next morning. We did not check during the afternoon, but he was present from dark until at least 0030 on 26 January, but was absent after sunrise on that day. We presume that a male may be on territory in the nesting colony for as long as 36 hours.

In contrast with highly territorial birds in the pre-egg stage, incubating birds may exhibit little territorial behavior. Although pre-egg territories may be vigorously defended, the nest scrape ultimately selected may be near the edge of the territory and within 1 or 2 m of an adjacent nest (pl. 5). Incubating birds seem to pay little attention to violent territorial contests and to intense courtship behavior within 1 to 2 m of their nests; even an intruder that comes within pecking range may get only a mild jab from an incubating bird. This low level of aggressiveness may be associated with the fact that adults have some difficulty locating their nests when they return from the coast after dark, and intense aggression by incubating birds toward intruders seeking their own nests would be a waste of energy as the latter do not pose a threat. Such intruders are sometimes chased or attacked by incubating or breeding birds, however, apparently depending on whether they approach in an aggressive posture or merely pass by in a nonaggressive attitude such as the Hunched Posture.

Unlike the usual situation in the coastal territories, aggressive behavior in the nesting colony sometimes leads to vigorous fights. These may be initiated by aerial pursuit (pl. 2) or by a flapping charge on the ground. The fights involve wing-flapping, tugging with locked bills, wing-pulling, and attempts to grasp the opponent's nape. Except for the sound of flapping wings, the fights are entirely silent.

The time of egg-laying varies from year to year. Goodall, Philippi, and Johnson found fresh eggs in the Pampa del Miraje colony on 22 November 1943. In the same area in 1968, Howell found no eggs until 11 December, and on 9 January 1970, about 13 months later, we found that egg-laying had barely begun and that only a single egg was present, if any, in most nest scrapes. Egg-laying is not synchronized in the colony either, for there was a spread of at least several weeks between the earliest and latest layers in 1970. These long-term and intracolony differences in timing are not likely to be caused by climatic conditions in the breeding area as these are virtually uniform from year to year. As we do not know the geographic sources of the breeding birds in this colony, we can make no inferences on the possible environmental stimuli that precisely determine reproductive timing.

We have data on the time of egg-laying in only three instances. In two of these an egg was present early in the morning which had not been there at sunset the preceding day, and in one instance an egg was laid about 1.5 hours

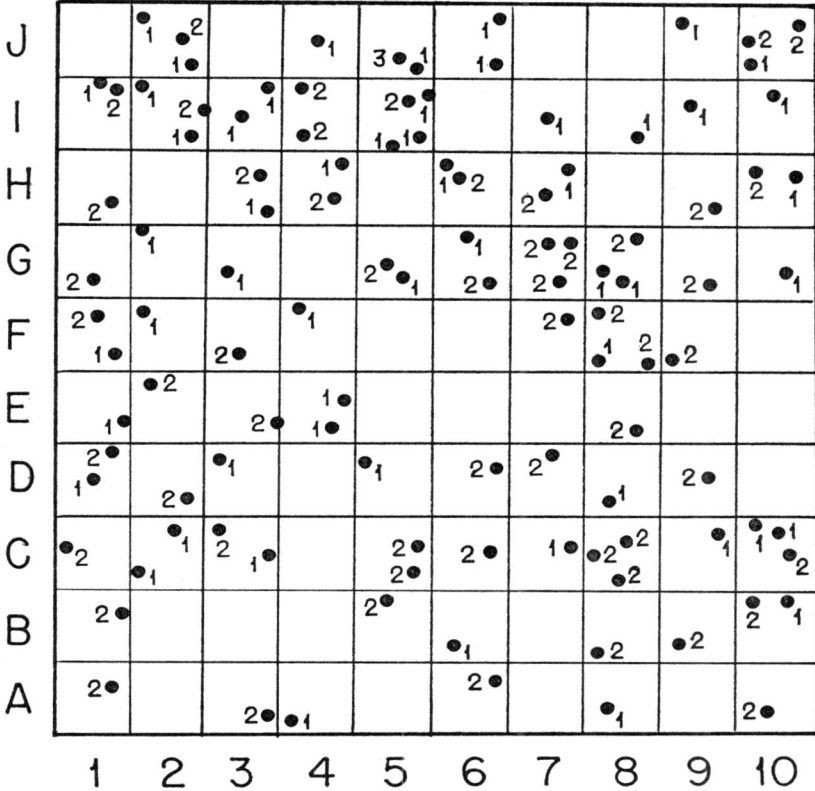

Fig. 3. Distribution of 110 Gray Gull nests with eggs in a 100 m x 100 m area; grid lines are at 10 m intervals. The number of eggs in each clutch is indicated, and the totals are: 1 egg, 54; 2 eggs, 55; 3 eggs, 1. The distribution within the entire plot does not differ significantly from that expected if random (see text).

after sunrise. We have no evidence that eggs are laid in the late morning or in the afternoon.

SIZE OF COLONY AND DISTRIBUTION OF NESTS

In 1943 Goodall, Philippi, and Johnson estimated the area of the Pampa del Miraje colony as 5 km^2. Twenty-seven years later we measured the long axis of the colony by odometer as 5.5 km and paced off the width at several intervals—driving a vehicle across it would have been too destructive. The width was fairly constant at about 1 km, giving a total area of 5.5 km^2, remarkably close to the 1943 estimate. Nests were not uniformly distributed throughout this area, and it is difficult to estimate accurately the number of pairs nesting there. We marked off an area 100 x 100 m (.01 km^2) in a well-populated part of the colony on 26 January 1970 and found 110 nests with eggs. The spatial distribution is shown in figure 3, and when the area is divided into 100 equal squares the number of nests per square varies from

0 to 4. The distribution of nests does not differ from that expected if spaced at random, as indicated by the fit of the points in the squares to a Poisson distribution. An equal density throughout the colony would mean 11,000 nests per km^2, or 60,500 nests in 5.5 km^2. Such a nesting density was definitely not present throughout the colony, and we estimate a total of about 10,000 nesting pairs.

As the substrate beyond the edges of the colony appears essentially identical with that within it, there is no reason to believe that soil conditions primarily determine the extent of the nesting area or the grouping of the nests. Although the spacing of nests in the 0.01 km^2 plot appeared to be random, the limitation of the entire colony to only a part of the available space exemplified clumping on a large scale. We found nests in every type of substrate in which a scrape could be made, from soft, powdery sand to moderately loose small stones. Only unyielding hardpan surfaces were not used, and disturbed soil was not necessarily avoided as one pair made its nest in one of our tire tracks. Our subjective impression is that areas of coarse sand with scattered small stones and nearby perching rocks were most favored, but many such areas remained unused.

There was another, much smaller colony of Gray Gulls in similar habitat 6 km SW of the main one. Howell visited the second colony on 3 December 1968 and found about 100 pairs; he saw some territorial behavior and fresh nest scrapes but no eggs. On 11 January 1970 we visited this colony and estimated that it included not over 100 pairs. Nest scrapes were sparsely distributed and seldom contained more than one egg, including some that were cold and evidently abandoned. We did not visit the small colony again and do not know the extent of its success or failure.

CLUTCH SIZE

A count of eggs in 182 nests known to be completed and attended showed 94 (52 percent) with two eggs, 85 (47 percent) with one egg, and 3 (1 percent) with three eggs. We examined hundreds of other nests and feel that the marked sample accurately represents the overall proportions within the entire colony. Most species of gull have predominantly three-egg clutches, but *Larus bulleri* of New Zealand also has a predominantly two-egg clutch (Beer, 1965), as does the Kittiwake, *Rissa tridactyla* (Cullen, 1957; Maunder and Threlfall, 1972). Only six nests with eggs of *L. fulginosus* of the Galápagos Islands have been reported and all had complete clutches of two (Snow and Snow, 1969). Data on all four species are shown in table 1. The small mean clutch size of *L. modestus* results from the almost equal number of one-egg and two-egg clutches. In the other species, two-egg clutches predominate overwhelmingly. Probably *L. modestus* has the smallest mean clutch size of any species of *Larus* and seems to be evolving from a presumably ancestral three-egg clutch toward the minimum of a single egg, as in the offshore-feeding Swallow-tailed Gull, *Creagrus furcatus*. The reduction in both these species seems surely related to the difficulty of raising young

TABLE 1
GULLS WITH SMALL AVERAGE CLUTCH SIZES

Species	1 egg		2 eggs		3 eggs		4 eggs		Mean	Source
	Number	Percent	Number	Percent	Number	Percent	Number	Percent		
L. modestus	85	47	94	52	3	1	0		1.55	This study
L. bulleri	260	28	565	61	97	10	6	<1	1.84	Beer (1965)
L. fuliginosus	0		6	100	0		0		2.00	Snow and Snow (1969)
Rissa tridactyla	21	15	104	75	13	10	0		1.90	Cullen (1957)
Rissa tridactyla (225 nests)	36	16	184 or 185	82	4 or 5	2	0		1.85	Maunder and Threlfall (1972)

in a severe environment and the need to travel long distances for food, as suggested by Lack (1967).

On 13 December 1968 Howell found two freshly dead adult males, each of which had two-part incubation patches in the pectoral region only (pl. 7). These birds had testes measuring 15 x 8 and 10 x 5 mm, respectively. On 11 January 1970 Araya found a fresh adult female that also had a two-part incubation patch. The cloacal opening was swollen and showed slight blood stains, indicating that an egg had recently been laid. The oviduct was much enlarged and the ovary included a yolked follicle 30 mm in diameter; the six next largest follicles were all about 5 mm in diameter. On 22 February we collected an adult male that was feeding two chicks about six to eight

TABLE 2
WEIGHTS (GRAMS) OF *Larus modestus* EGGS, ONE TO THREE DAYS POSTLAYING

	Number of eggs	Range	Mean	Standard Deviation	Standard Error of the Mean
One-egg clutch	43	42-62	52.6	4.75	0.72
Two-egg clutch					
Smaller egg	23	42-56	48.5	3.62	0.75
Larger egg	23	42-62	53.7	4.82	1.00
All eggs	89	42-62	51.8		

days posthatching, and he had a two-part incubation patch that showed emerging pinfeathers. This very small but random sample suggests that two-part patches are the rule in *L. modestus*, but this requires verification.

THE EGG

Johnson described the size and the color pattern of the egg, and there is considerable variation in the size, color, and density of the superficial markings. The ground color is notably pale compared with that of most other gulls (pl. 6), but it too is variable and often one egg is distinctly darker or paler than the other(s) in the same nest. A few eggs were almost white, with only a few faint markings. The size of eggs in the same nest is also variable, with one almost always noticeably smaller than the other. In each case in which we knew by marking which egg was laid first, the second egg was the smaller but might be either darker or about the same color. In one case we found that the third egg laid was smaller and darker than the previous two.

Weights of 89 fresh eggs are given in table 2. In only one of the two-egg clutches were the eggs of equal weight; the range of differences was 0 to 11 g with a difference in means of 5.2 g. The mean weights ± twice the standard error of the mean of the smaller and larger eggs in two-egg clutches do not overlap, but there is no statistically significant difference in the mean weight of one-egg clutches and that of the larger egg of two-egg clutches.

The weight of an adult female gull from the Pampa del Miraje colony was 370 g. The mean weight of all 89 eggs was 51.8 g, which is about 14 percent of the body weight of the female bird. If this percentage is typical, it is a relatively small figure according to the data of Lack (1967) and corresponds with the figures for offshore feeders that travel long distances from their nests for food.

Incubation necessarily begins with the laying of the first egg, for an egg could not safely be left uncovered during the hottest part of the day or during the near-freezing temperatures at night. If two eggs are laid, there is a two-day interval after the laying of the first—that is, the second egg appears on the third morning after the first egg.

LOCATION OF NEST BY RETURNING ADULTS AT NIGHT

The eye of the Gray Gull is proportionately no larger than that of any strictly diurnal gull but there is an eye-shine indicative of a diffuse reflective structure (pl. 8) which presumably improves vision in dim light. The Swallow-tailed Gull, which is largely nocturnal, apparently has a reflective optical structure that gives an eye-shine (Hailman, 1964), but that species has a relatively large eye. In the Gray Gull's nesting area the skies are always largely or completely clear so that starlight is bright enough to permit fair visibility at close range for the human eye, and the birds probably adjust their behavior to the necessity for close-range vision when there is no moon. From our blind we made many observations of birds that flew in and alighted right beside their nest and also of birds that alighted in the vicinity and walked around among several other nests before reaching their own. Of course, we have no way of knowing if the "direct arrivals" were really that or if there had previously been one or more erroneous site-locations beyond our field of vision. Often a bird arrived, approached several different birds on nests, and then departed; these could have been unmated birds or temporarily "lost" mates.

Vocalizations are surely important in mate-recognition and nest-site location, and during incubation and early stages of nestling care one mate is almost always at the nest site. The arrival of birds from the coast after dark is always accompanied by a mounting crescendo of gull cries, especially Long Calls, Long Call Notes, and Plaintive Long Call Notes. We often saw an incubating or brooding bird give a Long Call without rising from its nest, apparently in response to birds flying over, and possibly the flying birds recognize the calls of their own mates. An arriving bird may also give a Long Call just after alighting. Most such vocalizations sounded identical to our ears, but one member of a pair nesting beside our blind had a squeaky quality to its calls that we could readily recognize and the birds probably make much finer distinctions. Beer (1970b) found that Long Calls and the Ke-hah Call (= Plaintive Long Call Note?) are recognizably different among individuals of *L. atricilla* (see Discussion).

We saw so many variations in the behavior of birds participating in change-overs at the nest that we cannot describe any pattern as typical. At one extreme, a bird alights within 2-3 m of the nest, walks toward the incubating bird in Hunched or Low Oblique Posture; the latter stands, moves off a few steps, then flies away; the replacing bird then settles on the nest. No calls have been uttered. A more frequent pattern is as follows. A bird alights within a few meters of several nests, including its own. It walks toward one, and the sitting bird assumes an Upright Posture and utters several Aow or Kow notes, designated by Moynihan as the Plaintive Long Call Note. If the approaching bird comes within about 1.5 m, a Long Call may be given by the sitting bird. If the sitting and approaching birds are mates, the approaching bird assumes a Low Oblique Posture and gives Mew Calls; the sitting bird stands up, may or may not respond with Mew Calls, and walks off; the relieving bird settles on the nest. The relieved mate may fly off at once, or may walk farther away and fly off later, or may stay around or even return and go through a similar ceremony in attempting, successfully or not, to get back on the nest.

The arriving bird may approach several sitting birds in succession in Moderately Hunched Posture before finding its mate, and it usually moves away on hearing the Plaintive Long Call Notes of a bird other than its mate. Sometimes a bird approaches a sitter and at once goes into the Low Oblique–Mew Call pattern, with no Plaintive Long Call Notes uttered, or the Low Oblique–Mew Call pattern may be omitted.

The lack of uniformity and predictability in changeovers is shown by the following observation on the night of 21-22 January.

At 2340, an arriving bird approached a sitting one that gave a series of Plaintive Long Call Notes. During this, the approacher advanced rather hesitantly from one side, then the other, finally from the front, and the sitter concluded its vocalizations with a Long Call. The approacher then walked away. At 0015, the same sitting bird was approached by one that may or may not have been the same one as earlier. The sitter gave the same series of vocalizations, including a Long Call at the end, but the approacher this time circled around and crowded the sitter off the nest from the left rear. The relieved bird walked away about 7 m and remained quietly nearby for at least 15 minutes. In other instances, we saw sitting birds silently charge off the nest with wings raised and flapping at an approacher that came to within about 1.5 m.

These observations indicate that birds often have difficulty in recognizing their mates or nest sites at night. If the sitting bird does not recognize an approacher as its mate, it gives Plaintive Long Call Notes; possibly these are individually recognizable and discourage approach by nonmates but may provide a recognition signal to the mate. The latter bird may then "confirm" its identity by the Low Oblique–Mew Call pattern. "Confident" birds may simply approach quickly and silently whether or not the sitting bird vocalizes, but mistakes result in retreats or fights. According to Moynihan, the Plaintive Long Call Note is associated with conflict between attack and escape drives, and this would correspond to the sitting bird's situation if "departure" is substituted for "escape."

INCUBATION BEHAVIOR

Incubation behavior is closely coordinated with the daily climatic cycle in the colony. At dawn, with ambient temperature only a few degrees above 0°C, all incubating birds sit low and tightly on their eggs. They do not orient toward or away from the sun, but as the morning sun rises higher the posture of the birds becomes progressively less low and ground-hugging. By midmorning solar heat becomes intense and birds begin to ruffle their back and scapular feathers, providing additional insulation against insolation. At about this time, any nonincubating birds that may be present move off the ground and stand on the cooler surfaces of rocks. In midmorning this contingent comprises about 10 percent of the birds present and most appear to be mates of incubating birds as they often stand on a rock 1 to 1.5 m away from the latter (pl. 4). By midday and early afternoon, all incubating birds have risen and are standing over their nests shading the eggs. Their plumage is ruffled out maximally, with even the short feathers of the head and neck raised and the wings slightly abducted and drooped (pl. 9). Usually there is little or no wind, and any that blows comes from a northerly direction. Many birds also pant when the heat is most intense (pl. 10). The birds are still randomly oriented and the sun is almost directly overhead. In the early afternoon, without fail, the strong WSW wind begins suddenly. The exact time varies, but it is usually 7 or 8 hours after dawn and about 6 to 7 hours after sunlight reaches the nesting colony. The effect is dramatic, for within a few minutes all the birds turn and stand facing directly into the wind, still shading their eggs and with the plumage fully ruffled. The strong wind soon lowers the surface temperatures, and the birds begin to settle down on their eggs again. Ambient temperatures become progressively cooler, and by nightfall, when the WSW wind usually stops, the birds are once again tightly settled on their eggs.

No changeovers between mates are ever made during the day even if the nonincubating mate is present nearby. At night a bird may go off the nest for a few minutes for no apparent reason, perhaps from restlessness after many hours of continuous sitting or in association with the upsurge of activity as other birds arrive in the colony.

INCUBATION TEMPERATURES

To obtain incubation temperatures we bored a small hole in the large end of a fresh gull egg, inserted a fine vinyl-sheathed thermistor probe so that the tip approached the position of the embryonic disc, taped the exposed part of the probe to the egg shell, and placed the egg in an attended nest so that the probe tip was uppermost. By using long leads to our blind or vehicle, we could read within-egg temperatures directly from a Yellow Springs Instrument Company multichannel battery-powered thermistor thermometer. Other probes connected to different channels allowed simultaneous monitoring of a variety of ambient temperatures. Ideally this method gives an accurate approximation of the temperature of the embryo, but the incubating bird's movements may either rotate the egg and probe tip to the side or loosen and partly withdraw the probe. Low temperatures are therefore suspect, and the most reliable readings are those from a nest with a quietly sitting bird which show a steady rise and leveling off of egg temperature. In all cases one must check the position of the probe at the termination of the reading and discard records obtained from a displaced probe. The records in which we have greatest confidence show that at night, at ambient tem-

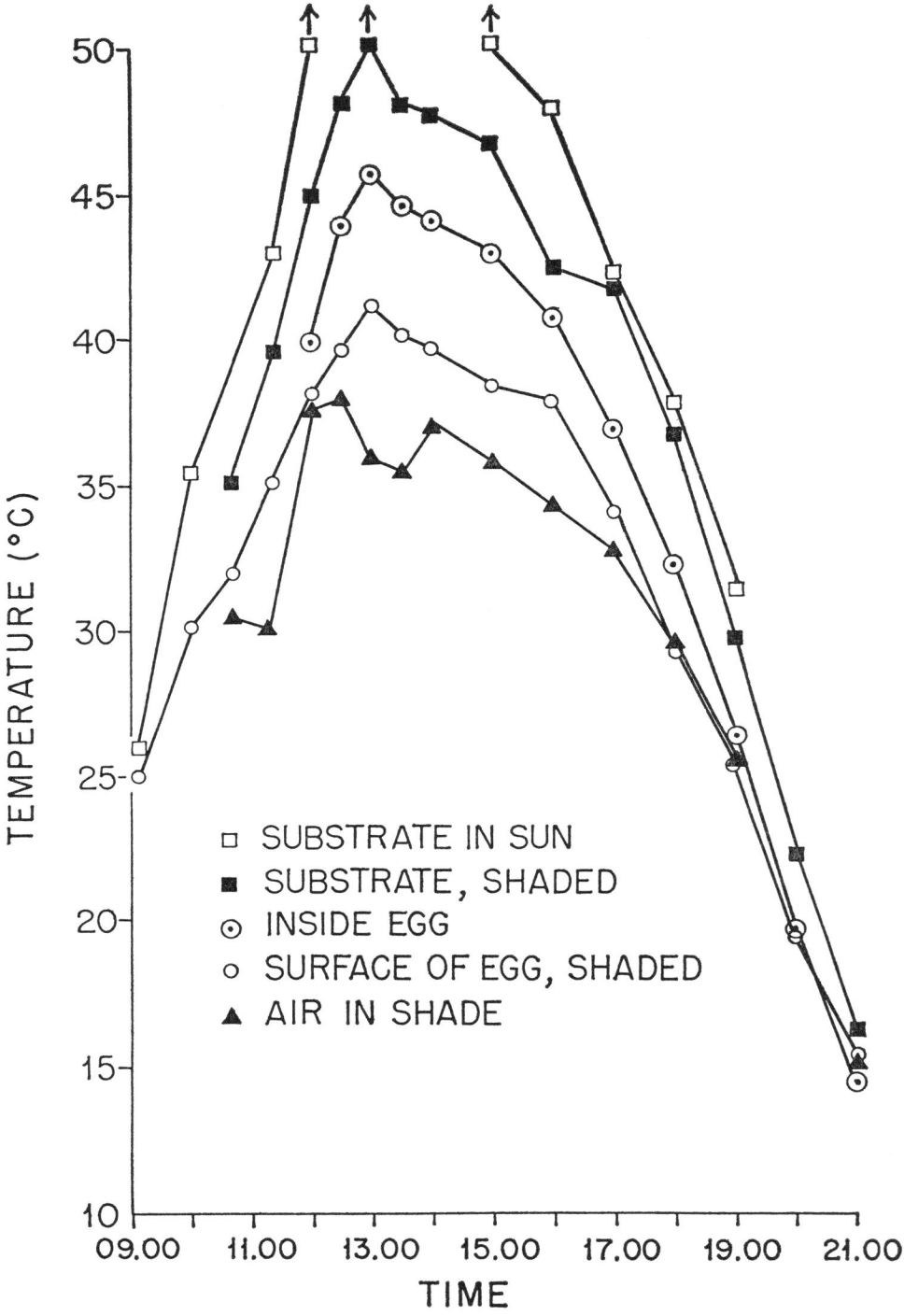

Fig. 4. Ambient and Gray Gull egg temperatures recorded in a nest scrape on 13 December 1968. Shaded substrate and egg surface temperatures were obtained by shading

peratures from 5-7°C, the steady incubation temperature is about 33° but egg temperature may drop 6-7° below that figure if the bird goes off the nest for a few minutes. During the day, egg temperatures are usually kept within about 35-37° whether the bird is sitting tightly or standing and shading the eggs. On 23 January, when a bird shading its egg went off the nest from 1332 to 1335 with full sun and no wind, the egg temperature rose during that three-minute interval from 37.1 to 39.0°.

Drent (1967), in a study of incubation in *L. argentatus,* suggested that an incubating bird under heat stress which rises and stands over its eggs may do so primarily to facilitate heat loss from its own body. The primary stimulus for such standing may be an adult comfort movement as Drent suggests, but it would also serve to prevent overheating of the eggs. Drent reports that a captive Herring Gull under heat stress reached a body temperature of 43°, and if incubation patch temperature were also at that level the eggs would become overheated if closely brooded. Whatever the motivation of the adult, shading of eggs in the Pampa del Miraje colony appears adequate to prevent overheating. Our highest recorded egg temperature of 38° was from a shaded egg, and the highest shaded air temperature at ground level that we recorded was 39.5° at 1300 on 13 December 1968, shortly before the afternoon WSW wind began. Most such air temperatures were well below 39°. Provided that the afternoon wind comes, as it invariably did during our stays in the colony, the egg temperature could closely approach the highest air temperature in the shade without risk of heat injury.

Drent (1967) recorded a mean of 37.6° ± .69° as the incubation temperature in the Herring Gull when the temperature-sensing probe was at the position of a 48-hour embryo. Our readings were taken under similar conditions, from fresh eggs probably no more than 2-3 days postlaying, but the usual daytime incubation temperatures were slightly lower than 37.6°. During the cold nights, the Gray Gull incubation temperature dropped to about 33° although the attending parent sits tightly almost all the time. Drent's measurements were presumably obtained during the day, and the mean minimum air temperature at night in his study area was about 10.5°C —considerably higher than that in the Pampa del Miraje.

Noting the large numbers of adult gulls on the coast during the nesting season and the pale color of the eggs, Johnson suggested that the eggs might not be continuously attended and that the pale eggshell might reflect enough solar heat to prevent overheating of uncovered eggs while the parents flew to the coast to feed. Johnson urged us to test this possibility as such an adaptation would be unique among birds. We found no evidence, either in 1968 or 1970, that such an adaptive pattern exists. The eggs are continuously covered by one or the other parent except for occasional periods of a few minutes.

---

the surface as the thermistor probe was applied to it. Symbols with upward-pointing arrows indicate readings above 50°, the upper limit of the instrument. The egg was fresh and a vinyl-sheathed thermistor probe was inserted through the large end so that the tip lay under the upper surface of the shell in the approximate position of the embryonic disc. Strong WSW wind began at about 1300 and continued throughout the afternoon. See text for other details of conditions and techniques.

We also performed experiments to see if a gull's egg would reach damaging or lethal temperatures if left in the sun. On 13 December, Howell placed a fresh gull egg and a fresh domestic hen's egg side by side in a nest scrape, each with an implanted thermistor probe and exposed to full sun and wind. As shown in figure 4, the temperature within both eggs reached levels above 44°C which are known to be lethal in eggs of domestic fowl. The gull egg (52 g) and the hen egg (54 g) were very similar in size, and the hen egg

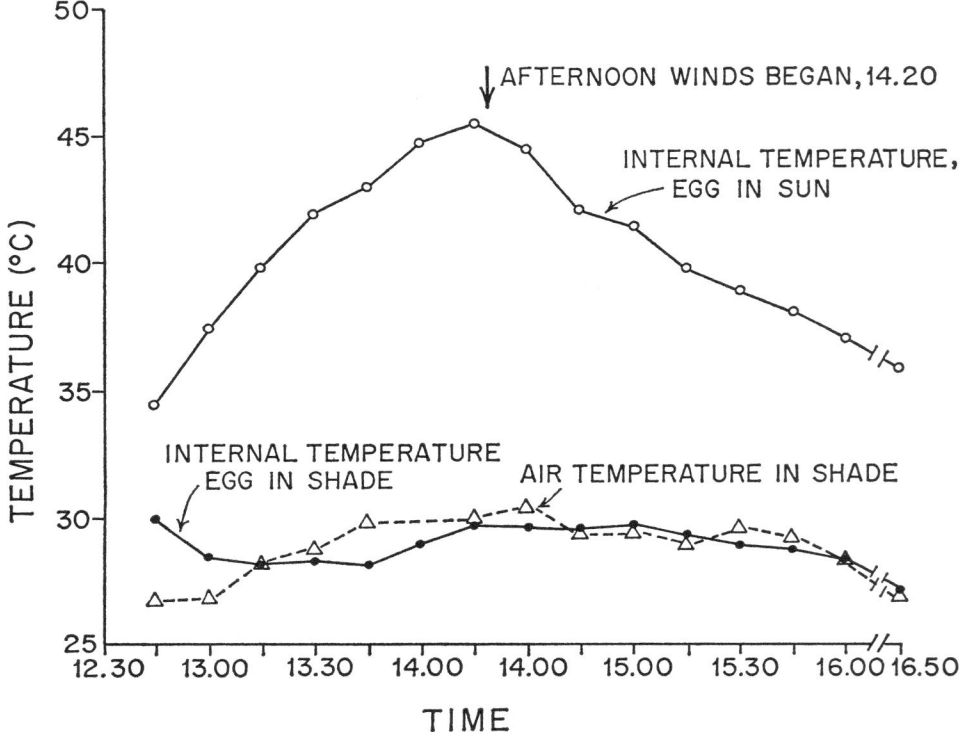

Fig. 5. Internal temperatures of fresh Gray Gull eggs in sun and shade and air temperature in shade, recorded on 26 January 1970. See text for details of experimental conditions.

maintained slightly lower surface and internal temperatures than the gull egg during the hotter parts of the day. On 26 January 1970 we performed a similar experiment when the air temperature was lower and the wind velocity and its effect could be measured. As figure 5 shows, the internal temperature of a gull egg in the sun eventually rose above 45° although air temperature stayed around 30°. After the afternoon wind began to blow steadily but moderately, egg temperature declined 9.6° in about 2.5 hours although air temperature dropped only 3° in the same period.

The span of incubation temperatures at which embryonic development proceeds normally has been thoroughly investigated only in the domestic fowl (Romanoff, 1960; review and summary). In that species the optimum span is from 35 to 39°C, with increasing incidence of abnormal effects at higher and lower temperatures according to the stage of embryonic development and duration of exposure. Our minimum and maximum steady incubation temperatures were 33 and 38°C, and this 5° span probably represents the optimal range for *L. modestus*. On a relatively mild day such as 26 January, there would be only two periods of about 2 hours each—from about 1100 to 1300 and about 1600 to 1800—when eggs left exposed would remain within that temperature range. As a flight from the coast to the nesting colony apparently requires about one hour (based on time of observed departure of flocks from the coast at dusk and arrival of birds in the nesting colony at least one hour after dark), two hours would not provide adequate time for a gull to fly to the coast, feed, and return without danger of damage to the eggs. Those birds that left their eggs for a longer period or were absent at the wrong time would suffer a drastic reduction in hatching success, and selection would therefore be rigorous for close attendance of the eggs.

Prevention of overheating or chilling appears to be the only advantage to virtually continuous covering of eggs. Most surprisingly, we never saw a Gray Gull attempt to eat an intact egg or make any gesture indicative of such an interest despite the exposure of scores of eggs each time we entered the nesting colony. We found circumstantial evidence that cracked eggs may be eaten but we saw this happen only once, when we accidentally broke an egg. Only a few other possible egg predators visit the nesting colony and these are discussed in a subsequent section.

INCUBATION PERIOD

We have only a few records of eggs marked on the day of laying and subsequently checked at the time of pipping and hatching. We found hundreds of eggs in the colony on 9 January 1970, but all those sampled were fresh and none had hatched by 26 January when we had to leave. All but three marked eggs of known age had hatched before our return on 16 February, and our most complete record is for a single egg that was laid close to our campsite sometime between darkness of 24 January and 0815 on 25 January. This egg was slightly pipped on 20 February, more fully pipped but not hatching by 1545 on 21 February, and fully hatched by 1400 on 22 February on the 29th day of incubation. A clutch of two was found and marked on 21 January; one egg was pipped on the morning of 17 February and fully hatched on the morning of 19 February. The second egg was pipped on the morning of 18 February and hatched between 0915 and 1500 on 20 February. Assuming that the last egg to hatch was laid on the morning of 21 January and the other on 19 January, these eggs hatched on the 31st and 32nd day of incubation, respectively. These figures indicate that the duration of the incubation is longer than that reported for other gulls of similar body size and egg weight (Lack, 1967; Vermeer, 1970).

Using Johnson's mean measurements for 14 Gray Gull eggs and using the formula (length x breadth^2 x 0.476) for the volume of gull eggs (Harris,

1964), the calculated mean volume of the egg of *L. modestus* is about 46.4 cc. Parsons's (1972) regression of calculated egg volume and incubation period for several European *Larus* species predicts an incubation period of between 24 and 25 days for an egg of that size or predicts an egg volume of over 90 cc. for an incubation period of more than 29 days. The Gray Gull's small egg and its incubation period of 29 days or more obviously do not conform to the pattern of these other species. Possibly this long incubation period is related to the relatively low nocturnal incubation temperatures of the Gray Gull (about 33°C).

THE CHICK

We found a two- to three-day interval between the earliest pip and full hatching in six instances for which we have adequate data. As there is a two-day interval between the laying of the first and second eggs, hatching is not synchronous and the second egg hatches one or two days after the first. This is different from the relatively synchronous hatching in some gulls (Barth, 1955; Drent, 1967). We have only three examples of marked two-egg clutches in which the time of hatching of each was known, but we often noted unmarked nests that included a fully hatched chick and a heavily pipped egg (pl. 11). Weights of five pipped eggs ranged from 38 to 42 g, and the newly hatched chicks weighed from 7 to 10 g less than the pipped egg. Weights of eight such chicks ranged from 31 to 38 g, with a mean of 34 g. In two instances for which we have data, the weight of the second chick at hatching was 3 or 4 g less than the hatching weight of the first. This is consistent with evidence that the second egg is smaller than the first, and presumably the smaller chick would have less chance of survival in case of a shortage of food. In one case among our marked birds the second chick to hatch lost weight steadily and died although still in the nest scrape with its older sibling, but among many others both chicks were gaining weight in the first few posthatching days when we were able to monitor them. Certainly we saw no indication that the younger chick usually perishes as in some boobies (Sulidae).

In one instance we saw an adult gull pick up an eggshell from its nest and fly off and drop it, but we do not know if this is the usual behavior. In any case the afternoon wind would soon blow eggshells out of nest scrapes.

The down of newly hatched chicks is pale gray to buffy, with spots of black or gray primarily on the dorsal surfaces but also on the flanks, sides of head, and throat (pl. 12). Although some chicks are distinctly buffy, the pale grayish tone prevails in most. Spotting ranges from moderate to dense, and no chicks were sparsely spotted although the degree of paleness varies. The outlines of the spots are usually not sharply defined, and these blurry markings give the patterning a slightly "smoky" quality. The legs and feet are gray, and the bill is dark gray over the proximal two-thirds and pinkish gray at the distal one-third, with a white egg tooth that persists for two to four days. The mouth lining is bright pink. As the chicks grow larger the markings become even less distinct, and by the time they weigh more than

200 g the general appearance is pale gray with blurry mottling of darker gray (pl. 21). All ages of young birds that we saw generally matched the grayish color of the substrate.

NESTLING CARE

A parent bird is always at the nest during the first posthatching day and usually for the next several days, but adults are less likely to brood young chicks as continuously as they incubate eggs. When an adult is standing over the nest or if the adult is absent, chicks of any age may wander out of the nest scrape in random directions. Although this often exposes young chicks to the risk of death from overheating, the parent birds never move away from the nest scrape to shade or brood a chick. Thus, an adult that left its nest long enough for a small chick to wander away returns only to the nest scrape and never to its chick even if the latter is in plain sight only a few centimeters away exposed fully to the midday sun. Furthermore, adults often move out and attack any chick, including their own, which approaches within a few meters of the nest. The attack consists of sharp pecks that often send tufts of down flying, and the reaction of the chick is the same as that described as Beak-hiding in the Kittiwake by Cullen (1957) and as the Bill-down Crouch by Moynihan (1959a). The chick crouches low and points its bill down, in extreme cases tucking it under the body so that the bill points posteriorly and the nape, not the crown, is most exposed (pl. 15). There are no especially conspicuous markings on the nape, as there are in Kittiwake chicks. This submissive or appeasement posture seems to blunt the aggressive drive of the adult and it soon stops attacking. After a few minutes the chick gradually raises its head and eventually advances again toward the nest. Often there are several attack-submission sequences before the chick finally gets under the adult and into the scrape. As soon as the chick is under the adult, the latter's behavior immediately changes from aggression to broodiness. It may touch the chick gently with its bill, which shows that it is aware of its presence and has not stopped attacking merely because the chick got out of sight. In contrast with this typical behavior, an adult sometimes shows no aggression toward its own or another chick less than 1 m away, or the adult may come off its nest and attack a quiet stationary chick several meters away for no apparent reason. We saw many attacks on chicks but none seemed seriously injured except in the case of one particularly persistent aggressive adult that killed at least one chick. It is likely, however, that chicks may be weakened or killed by exposure to intense sun when attacks prevent them from reaching shade during the critically hot hours. We never saw an adult attempt to eat a chick although this is common practice among many other gull species.

An important aspect of the adult-chick relationship is that chicks of various ages often try to get under an adult that is not the chick's own parent and which is away from the chick's nest. Any adult will accept, brood, and may even feed any chick that manages to get under it and into that adult's nest. Fostering of chicks is shown in varying degrees by many species of gulls, but it seems especially prevalent in *L. modestus*. Even if the bird's own chick(s) are present, and even if the visitor is considerably older and larger or younger and smaller than the resident chick, the visitor is accepted. This behavior is best illustrated by the following edited paraphrase from Howell's field notes of 22 February on adult "B," attending a nest with a 45 g chick about 5 days old and an egg that never hatched.

At 0910, B's own chick had wandered off about 2 m from its nest and had settled in the open in full sun. B remained sitting on its egg and then went to sleep, with its head tucked into its scapular feathers. At 1015 two chicks that were an estimated 8 to 10 days old and weighed about 50 and 80 g, respectively, approached to within 1.5 m of B who was now awake. B half-stood and gave a Long Call. Immediately the larger of the two chicks ran up and got under B, into the nest scrape, without being attacked. The chick then solicited feeding by nibbling at B's bill. B did not bring up food but gave a moaning Mew Call, went into Choking, and then aggressively but rather gently pecked the larger chick that persisted in soliciting feeding. B moved toward the smaller chick; the larger followed and was pecked as it tried to get under B. B again went into Choking, giving Mew Calls. The smaller chick then came up to B and was pecked; the two chicks were now on either side of B, both in Beak-hiding submissive posture. B gave two Long Calls and gently pecked the smaller chick and then the larger one. B then returned to its nest 1.5 m away, gave a Long Call, and settled. About 5 minutes later, at 1025, the larger chick again came up as B stood beside its nest and got under it and then got into the nest as B moved on to it. B's own chick still had not moved from its position 2 m away. At 1040, chick B had moved to within 1 m of another nest and the brooding adult came over and attacked it; chick B went into full Beak-hiding Posture with its head turned under its breast. At 1053 chick B roused and moved to about 1.5 m of its own nest, within sight of adult B. At 1101 B was standing, shading the large chick, and gave a Long Call but its own chick did not move. At 1120 chick B got up and started toward its nest, stopping about 0.75 m away. Adult B assumed an Upright Posture and gave several Plaintive Long Call Notes. Chick B stopped, turned away, and began picking up and swallowing very small pebbles. It gradually moved closer to the nest, and B assumed a Low Oblique Posture, gave a Mew Call, and then gave a Long Call. Chick B went into Beak-hiding Posture, then stood up and with a few steps tumbled into the nest at 1124. Adult B remained standing over the nest, shading chick B, the larger chick, and the egg.

Although adult B did not attack its own chick on this occasion, on 20 February the adult went off the nest and strongly pecked chick B at several stages of its gradual progress back toward its nest. We saw other instances from the blind of parental attacks on their own chicks when the latter were outside the nest.

We find it difficult to interpret adult B's behavior beyond saying that the bird was experiencing conflicting drives toward aggressive and parental activity, and that its displays signaled territoriality and perhaps its individual identity (see Discussion). The chicks appear to be motivated only toward shade and feeding, and whether or not an adult that may provide these is their own parent seems not to matter. If attacked, the chick does not flee but assumes a submissive posture until the attack is over, then seeks shelter or food again. Moynihan (1959a) described "Burrowing" of chicks under adults when attacked, but Gray Gull chicks sometimes get under a nonparent without being attacked, as documented above.

The wandering habits of the chicks made it almost impossible to be certain which chick belonged to which nest unless the chicks were marked just after hatching. Our activities contributed to the confusion, for our visits to the blind always flushed the adults and chicks often scattered also. Daily weighings caused considerable chick movement, and the blind itself altered the situation by providing an abundance of shade during the day or shelter from the nightly cold. Often two or three chicks came into the blind and stayed for many hours, and marked birds made repeated visits. Despite all this, most marked chicks consistently returned to the nest scrape which we knew or inferred to be their own. We marked 12 chicks in nests that were visible from the blind and attempted to keep track of them. One of these weighed 57 g on the morning of 18 February, when we found it close to but not in a marked nest scrape. On 20 February it was in a different nest; on 21 February it was in the scrape near which it was first marked; on 22 February we could not find it; on 23 February it was in still another nest, its third. By the latter date its weight had increased to 79 g. Several times we found two or three chicks in nests that had had clutches of one or two eggs, respectively, and we often saw incidents like that given in detail above for nest B, in which a chick solicited food or sought shade from an adult that was not its parent. Usually the adult approached was attending another chick, but we never saw any aggression among the chicks. On two occasions we saw adults feed a chick that we could tell was not the adult's own at that adult's nest site, and on other occasions we saw adults feed chicks that were probably but not demonstrably not their own. This behavior involved chicks of ages up to at least 10 days, beyond the time at which some other species of larids achieve parent-offspring recognition (Beer, 1969; Evans, 1970).

In totality this adult-chick behavior appears paradoxical. The aggressive actions of adults toward chicks—even their own—may force the young birds to be exposed to potentially fatal heat stress. Yet, by accepting any chick that manages to get itself under them, the adults probably contribute to the survival of chicks that might not be able to reach shelter in time. Around midday the only effective shade is that provided by adult birds, and acceptance of visiting chicks may lead to greater total survival of chicks at no cost to the adult bird or to its own brood. Although a chick may lose some food to a hungry visitor, the deprived chick may compensate by obtaining food another time from a different adult. Another possible explanation is that parents and chicks may not always locate each other at night, when most feeding is done, and opportunistic feeding may be advantageous. It is surprising that the chicks are not as strongly attached to the nest scrape as are the adults, as such site fixation would virtually eliminate the dangers of overexposure or underfeeding. The fact that adults may accept chicks other than their own does not necessarily mean that either adults or chicks are incapable of individual recognition. There seem, however, to be few vocal signals exchanged between adults and young birds. Newly hatched and very young chicks often give soft, single-note cheeps, but these notes are so simple that we doubt that they could be used to distinguish individuals and in any case they are usually given when the chick is unattended. Chicks do not regularly vocalize when an adult arrives after an absence, and adults seldom direct vocalizations toward chicks. Our impression is that young chicks may cheep when they are hungry or uncomfortable, whether or not an adult is present, but this does not seem to attract adults or get a noticeable response from them. Chicks older than about 10 days have a repeated three-note call— chee-chee-chee—that seems to indicate hunger. This call is louder than the cheep notes but is still not very noisy and almost never seems to attract adults. Adults have no calls given exclusively to chicks. As mentioned, adults may give a Long Call, Plaintive Long Call Note, or a Mew Call from Low Oblique Posture when approached by a chick. Sometimes a Mew Call is given just before an adult disgorges food for a chick. Rarely we heard an adult give a Long Call Note at its nest that seemed to attract chicks to it, but this was uncorrelated with either stressful temperature or aggression or feeding. Possibly adults use vocal signals when the young are larger and may wander farther from the nest site, but we have no evidence that this happens and saw no indication that adults "call in" younger chicks for brooding or feeding.

FOOD

The young are fed primarily or perhaps entirely on fish, for we did not recognize anything else among many feedings observed and disgorged samples examined. On 22 February we collected an adult male at 2240 as he arrived at his nest site. The bird's total weight was 400 g; the lower esophagus and proventriculus were packed with fish muscle and these organs and their contents weighed 53 g. There were no fins, tails, heads, or large bones in the solid mass of fish so that virtually all would have been digestible. The gizzard was empty except for about eight pebbles 3 to 4 mm in diameter, and we estimate that the bird was carrying about 40 g of food.

An adult coming in from the coast at night usually feeds the chick(s) almost at once or within a few minutes after arriving at the nest. Chicks solicit feeding by nibbling rapidly at the adult's bill, and the adult goes into a Low Oblique Posture (pl. 18) and disgorges a mass of food that is only a portion of the entire amount carried. The adult's bill is black without any markings, but it contrasts sharply with the white head even in dim light and thus forms an easily visible target at night. The food mass is dropped on the ground and the chicks quickly eat it there or seize bites as it is disgorged. Sometimes an adult holds a lump of food in its bill while the chick pecks at it, and sometimes the adult reswallows some of it. If there is more than one chick, each eats independently of the other and without conflict, although larger chicks are naturally at an advantage in getting the most. We have one record of a day-old chick weighed after its first feeding, and it had gained 6 g. Portions eaten by older chicks are larger, but we have no figures. Occasionally an adult disgorged food without solicitation by the chick, and rarely the adult gives a Mew Call before bringing up the food mass.

The nocturnal feeding after the adult arrives from the coast is the only one that is reasonably predictable. The same bird that comes in at 2200 may

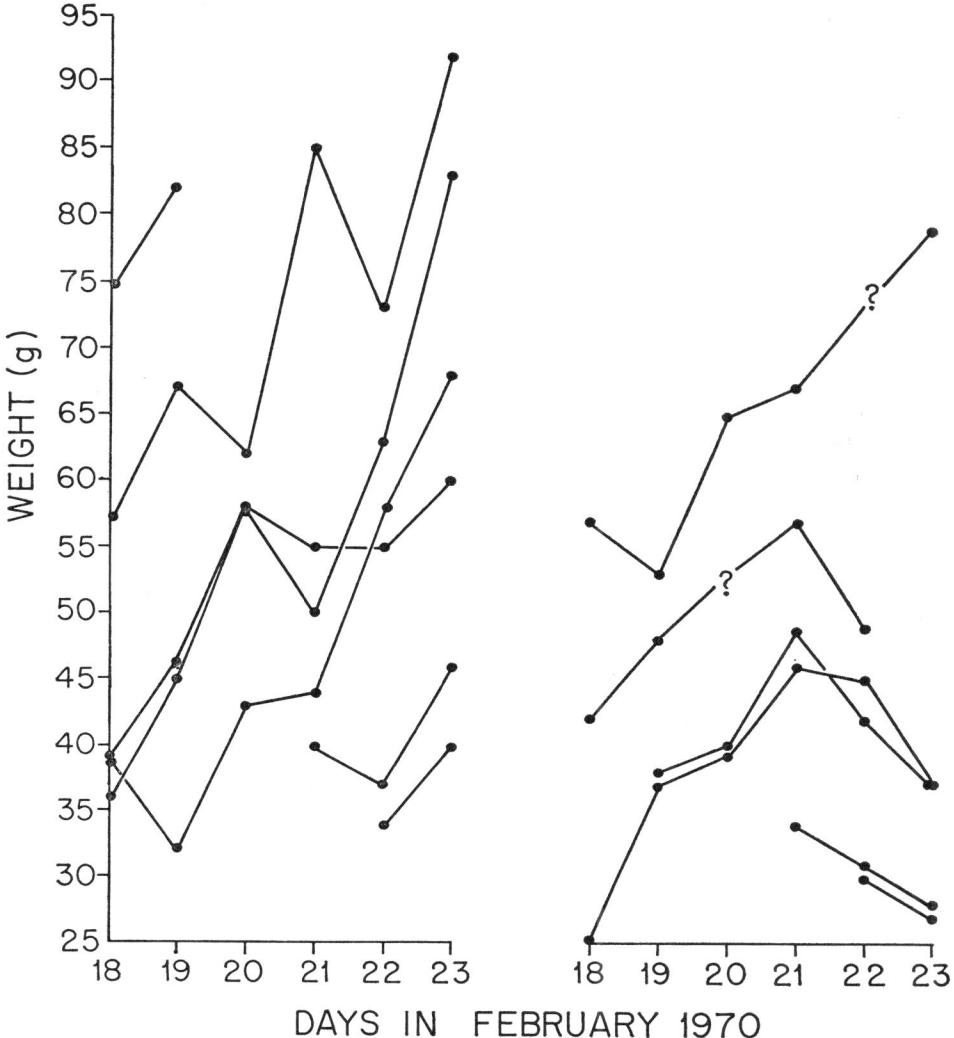

Fig. 6. Growth rates of Gray Gull chicks, divided for graphic clarity into groups that had increased (left) or decreased (right) at their last weighing. The exception in the right group is a chick that was found in three different nest scrapes on different mornings and was not located on 22 February. All weighings were done between 0800 and 0930.

give several feedings during the night and the following day, but we saw none later than late afternoon and never any in the early evening. Feedings are not always at the nest scrape, but those that we saw were probably not more than 1-2 m away from it. There may be a slight peak of feeding at dawn, but this is uncertain. Often an adult retches but fails to bring up any solid food even though some may be disgorged at a later time. If the roughly 40 g of food carried by the bird collected on 22 February was a typical

GROWTH OF CHICKS

From 18 to 23 February we weighed marked chicks between the hours of 0800 and 0930, when any nocturnal and dawn feedings would have been completed. As chicks get older they are increasingly difficult to locate and capture as they run rapidly and far, and when caught they may disgorge their stomach contents. Our records are therefore not as extensive as we would like, but the great disturbance caused by more chasing of chicks would have yielded data of dubious precision and might have caused extensive desertion and mortality.

The data for as many as six consecutive morning weighings (fig. 6) show wide variability and indicate that growth is very rapid under favorable circumstances. No chicks, however, showed a continuous weight increase without interruption by at least one record of no gain or of a loss. Nonfeeding or underfeeding may result from a failure of one parent to return at night or from the absence of the chick at the nest when the parent arrives so that a sibling or a visiting chick gets most or all of the food provided during the night. The slopes of the curves showing weight loss are sufficiently similar to suggest that each decline results from nonfeeding over the preceding 24 hours. Although adults usually changed places at night at the nests we could see from the blind, we feel sure that sometimes the mate that was absent during the day did not return during the following night. This is difficult to determine with certainty as it requires an all-night watch with no interruption and unfailing attention and good visibility. During a watch interrupted by shifts among ourselves, we failed to detect a changeover at nest A on the night of 21 February, and at 0810 on 22 February chick A weighed 73 g, a loss of 7 g since a weighing at 2045 the previous evening. On our one continuous all-night watch from a vehicle on 24-25 January, before any eggs hatched, we noted birds changing over at nests at 0145 and 0430 although most exchanges occurred before midnight. On 23 February at 0825, while weighing chicks, we saw a large circling columnar flock of about 100 birds over the southwest part of the nesting colony. As we watched, the birds peeled off one by one and glided gradually downward toward the nesting colony. Araya saw a similar event at about 1000 on 22 February. It is likely that the flock was a group of birds arriving from the coast in the morning, perhaps individuals that had not come in at all the night before, and this may be more frequent as chicks get older. Unfortunately, we had to leave the colony on 23 February and had no chance to check this possibility.

As we were not able to mark newly hatched chicks earlier than 18 February we had no marked chicks of a known age greater than 6 days by our departure on 23 February. As weights vary considerably according to feeding schedules, body weight gives only a general indication of age. Beyond a certain age, chicks may be left unattended by adults for much or all of a day, and we estimate this age as about 8 days and beyond. Such long-unattended chicks weigh at least 80 g if well fed, or more than 20 percent of adult weight, but some may weigh as little as 55 g. Probably no chicks are regularly left alone for the entire day until they are of more than 100 g size, and such older chicks tend to assemble in small groups. For example, at midafternoon on 22 February, all 12 adults visible within 15 m in front of the blind were sheltering chicks and there were no "unemployed" adults. Within the same area, unattended chicks comprised one group of four chicks, two groups of three, three groups of two, and four solitary ones. This contrasts with the situation during incubation, when all eggs are covered by adults and approximately 10 percent more nonincubating adults are present. Presumably the much greater energy demands of chick care require longer absences for food-gathering by adults.

Eight chicks of ages estimated as one to several days which were found dead in fresh condition were prepared as study skins. The gut of the smallest ones contained some yolk, and the stomachs of all contained from a few to more than 50 small pebbles about 2-5 mm in diameter. We often saw chicks picking up and swallowing pebbles either during the day or at night. Some stomachs contained a brown paste that felt and smelled like oily fish.

THERMOREGULATION

Most young chicks get into the shade under an adult during the hotter times of day, and the standing, wing-drooped heat-stress posture of the adults provides shade and full exposure to wind for the chicks (pl. 13). Larger chicks also seek shade under adults, even those so large that they can barely fit under the adult's body. When an adult is standing on a rock, one or two larger chicks often manage to clamber up on the rock and get into the shade (pls. 14, 16). Unattended chicks older than about 10 days often stand alone on rocks in the manner of adults, perhaps conditioned to do so by shade-seeking under rock-standing adult birds. These chicks may let their wings droop considerably, but as the remiges are barely beginning to show it seems doubtful that this posture contributes much to heat dissipation.

We conducted two experiments to test the ability of young birds to maintain body temperature below the lethal level in full sun both before and after the afternoon wind had begun. On 18 February, we gathered 10 chicks that weighed from 27 (first posthatching day) to 226 g (with contour feathers showing on major tracts). At 1020 these were placed in a corral made of piled-up stones enclosing about 1 m^2, and deep esophageal temperatures were taken at intervals with a thermistor thermometer probe until 1315. Air temperature in the shade and temperatures of soil that was in the sun but shaded as the probe was applied to it were recorded at similar intervals. Between 1040 and 1130 some wispy light clouds occasionally drifted across the sun and there were sporadic light breezes from the northeast, but after 1130 the sun was unobscured and there was no wind. Results are shown in figure 7. The smallest chick, (no. 1) did not go directly to shade but simply moved about and stopped at random. If it encountered another bird the small chick attempted to get under it, but we prevented this. Its body temperature

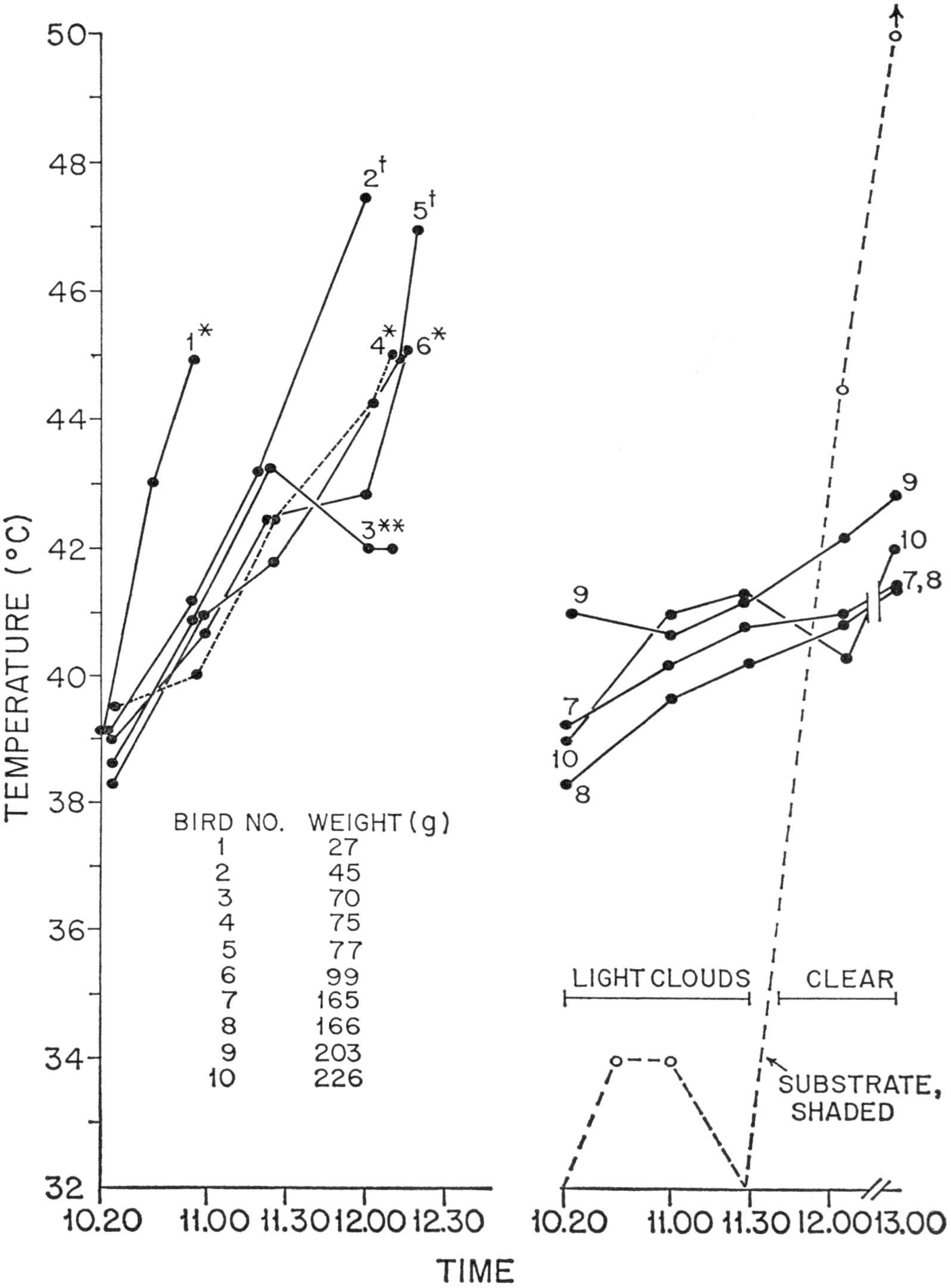

Fig. 7. Ambient and body temperatures of young Gray Gulls exposed to sun in still air on 18 February 1970. Air temperature in shade varied from 25.2 to 30.2°C. For graphic

rose rapidly to 45.0° and it would undoubtedly have died had we not removed it to shade, after which it soon recovered completely. The stone corral cast enough shade for the intermediate-sized chicks (nos. 2-6) to get partly out of the sun, and we tethered them by fastening their legs together with tape and put them in full sun. These birds struggled sporadically, which undoubtedly raised their heat production, and they panted vigorously. Despite our attempts to detect the time of critical hyperthermia and to remove overstressed birds to shade, numbers 2 and 5 reached body temperatures of 47.5° and 47.0° and died. Numbers 4 and 6 reached 45.0° and 45.1° and were removed to shade and recovered. Number 3 managed to get into partial shade — enough, apparently, to keep its temperature at safe levels. All the larger birds (nos. 7-10) huddled together and got some shade from one another but the body contact may have offset this advantage by diminishing convective heat loss. They kept their body temperatures well below the lethal level for almost 3 hours and panted only at intervals and not continuously.

The data indicate that only chicks well over 100 g in weight are able to thermoregulate with little or no shade and in still air for the several hours during which ambient temperatures approach peak levels. Under the same conditions, smaller chicks probably need at least partial or occasional shade, and the smallest chicks are vulnerable to even one hour of severe heat stress when there is no wind.

On 21 February at 1445 we took deep esophageal temperatures of two small chicks sharing the same nest site, exposed to full sun and to the brisk afternoon wind. They weighed 31 and 60 g and were probably one and three days old. We confined them to the nest site by surrounding them with stones on all sides except one open to the wind and recorded temperatures at 10-minute intervals for 30 minutes, with the results shown in table 3. The smaller chick attempted to get its head into shaded crevices of our rock fence but could not get more than about one-eighth of its dorsal surface out of the sun. Both birds panted vigorously and almost constantly. Although the temperature in still air was higher than that recorded in the earlier experiment, these small chicks were well able to maintain a safe body temperature in full sun because of the cooling effect of the wind. The data suggest that even a one-day-old chick could be left unattended once the afternoon wind started without danger of overheating, but dehydration might become a serious problem under those conditions.

Once they have been fed, chicks of all ages have a white crust distal to their nostrils which indicates functioning nasal salt-excreting glands (pl. 12). In addition to disposing of any excess salt taken in with food, these glands may aid in water conservation by reducing the need for water to carry away salt

---

clarity, temperatures of birds weighing less than 100 g are plotted on the left and those of larger birds are on the right, but all birds were simultaneously exposed to the same conditions. See text for details of experimental procedures.

* removed to shade; survived
** in partial shade after 1130
† died

excreted by the kidneys, which cannot concentrate salt as greatly as can the nasal glands.

MORTALITY AMONG YOUNG BIRDS

The largest chick that we weighed was a 226 g bird on 18 February, but one captured at the same time which weighed 203 g was more advanced in plumage growth. In this bird the wing coverts and remiges are just erupting from their sheaths, and the feathers along the ventral tract are fully unsheathed. No rectrices are visible, and only a few contour feathers appear under the down on the head. By 23 February we saw many young birds that appeared to be as much as two weeks beyond that stage, but all were still largely covered with down and none were close to having fully grown flight feathers.

TABLE 3
THERMOREGULATION OF CHICKS IN SUN AND WIND
(Temperature in °C)

Time	1445	1455	1505	1515
Air temperature in shade shielded from wind	35.5	35.5	34.5	35.0
Soil temperature in wind, immediately after shading	45.5	—	44.0	45.0
Wind speed	Varied from 6.1 to 10.2 miles per hour			
Body temperature of 31 g chick	42.0	43.0	42.0	42.0
Body temperature of 60 g chick	42.2	42.0	42.0	40.8

The young of the Gray Gull have no source of food except that brought by adults, and the juveniles must be fed until they are able to fly well enough to reach the coast 30 km away. Unlike the young of most other gull species, they cannot walk or clumsily fly a short distance from the nest site to a nearby lake or seashore. We do not believe that juveniles could survive a strenuous journey of more than a few hours in the barren Pampa del Miraje. As it is extremely unlikely that adults would shelter and feed them en route, we think that juveniles must be cared for in the nesting colony until able to make long flights, and this care probably lasts at least 40 days. As we were unable to remain at the nesting colony beyond 23 February, we have no data on the care of more advanced young birds and this remains an intriguing subject for future investigation.

There is no doubt, however, that mortality is high among young birds of all ages. As it would have been impossible to obtain precise figures without greatly increasing mortality through disturbance, we can only make qualitative statements. We often found dead chicks one or a few days old in nest scrapes or away from them, including areas not previously visited by us. Freshly dead chicks of older ages might be found anywhere, including within our blind. As none that we examined had any externally apparent injuries, we presume that they died of starvation or exposure or a combination of these.

Parasites or disease may possibly cause some of this mortality, but we saw no birds with a sickly or diseased appearance. We handled many live young birds and a few recently dead adults and noticed no ticks or other ectoparasites. Internal parasites usually go through a cycle lasting at least several days before causing the death of the host (if this occurs), and such infestations are not likely to be responsible for mortality of very young chicks. Disease may be involved, but the relatively sterile desert environment does not appear favorable for the spread of pathogenic microorganisms although direct transmission of these from parent to offspring could occur. From the available evidence, we believe that heat stress and starvation are the most probable major causes of mortality among chicks and juveniles.

The entire colony was littered with dried carcasses of young birds of all ages, including advanced juveniles, from some previous year. We found no carrion-eating insects in the desert, and carcasses dry to mummified condition. Most date back at least one year, some perhaps much more. The strong wind blows these mummies about, and accumulations of them in certain places are probably fortuitous and not necessarily evidence of crèches that perished together.

PREDATION

Although mortality appears high in young birds of all ages, the effect of predation in the nesting colony seems insignificant. Our data indicate that, other than man, there are only four actual or potential predators on the Gray Gull and its eggs in the desert. These four are the only other species of vertebrates that we found in the nesting colony — the Andean Condor *(Vultur gryphus)*, Turkey Vulture *(Cathartes aura)*, Peregrine Falcon *(Falco peregrinus)*, and a fox *(Dusicyon sp.)*. We doubt that the condor has any important impact as we seldom saw one over the colony and never saw one alight. Nevertheless, on 22 January a condor cruised over the colony less than 100 m above ground and caused an upflight of about 100 birds. From one to three gulls harassed it by swooping from behind, but as the condor soared above about 100 m they gave up the chase.

Turkey Vultures were almost always present over the colony during the daylight hours, with up to 20 in view at times. They rarely came down to the ground, but when they did there was panic among the gulls in that vicinity. We did not see Turkey Vultures eating eggs but have circumstantial evidence that they sometimes do as we found a few punctured and eaten eggs where these vultures had been. As we never saw a gull eat an intact egg despite innumerable opportunities, we presume that Turkey Vultures must have done so. This seems a relatively rare occurrence, however, for we seldom saw the vultures on the ground and the number of eggs eaten must be very small. Oddly, we never saw vultures come down and eat dead chicks of any size, but they do feed on dead adults. Stephen E. Chapman of Southampton, England, who visited the Pampa del Miraje colony the following year, has data showing, however, that egg predation and scavenging by Turkey Vultures was much more prevalent during the 1971 nesting season (pers. comm.).

In both 1968 and 1970 a single Peregrine Falcon was frequently present around the colony. In each year the bird was an adult of the North American subspecies *anatum;* quite possibly it was the same individual, and for convenience we shall write of it as such. We never saw it catch a gull but several times it made passes at single birds or over a flock that it scared up. Our impression was that it could easily have struck a gull at any time despite surprisingly agile maneuvers by the latter, and the falcon sometimes seemed to play at causing panic flights of gulls. One freshly dead adult gull had puncture wounds on its back that may have been caused by a falcon strike, but the bird was not plucked or eaten.

Parenthetically, an adult *F. p. anatum* was a regular visitor to a radio tower on the rocks in front of the Hotel Antofagasta. This bird often swooped down and panicked hundreds of gulls of several species, including *L. modestus,* but always passed by the gulls to strike one of a few domestic pigeons *(Columba livia)* that came to pick at scraps along the beach.

We found footprints of a small canid on 17 February, and as there were no domestic dogs in the area we assumed that the tracks were those of a fox *(Dusicyon),* the only wild canid that occurs in the region. On 18 February we found an old desiccated carcass of a juvenile fox and saved the head for identification (UCLA no. 19293). O. P. Pearson examined the specimen and informs us that it is not certainly identifiable to species and may be either *Dusicyon griseus* or *D. culpaeus.* When the gulls are not nesting there is no sustenance for a fox in this desert, but at the right season wandering individuals from the coast or from along the Río Loa might locate the gull colony by the noise at night. Several times we noted panicky upflights at night long after one of us had settled in the blind, and these may have been caused by a fox although we never saw or heard one. Our most certain evidence of fox predation was a fresh-appearing scat made up mostly of feathers, including down, and small bone fragments. We would surely have seen fox tracks more than once and found more scats if foxes regularly ranged through the colony, and carcasses of adult gulls were seldom found by us. Our data suggest that foxes are only occasional predators and of minor importance.

NOCTURNAL ACTIVITY OF ADULTS ON THE COAST

On 19 January we camped on the beach at Hornito, 84 km north of Antofagasta. This locality is almost due west of the Cerro de Colupo and thus represents the coastal area closest to the nesting colony, which at that time had many complete clutches but as yet no hatchings. The beach at Hornito is largely sandy but there are some rocky places and small rock islets. In the afternoon there were several hundred Gray Gulls near our campsite, many of them probing for *Emerita* in the wash of the waves. They were generally active and vocal on the beaches, the rocks, and on the water until dusk, at which time they began to drift away. There was no large circling flock, and the trend of movement was northward along the coast, not directly east toward the desert. By 2130 all sunlight was gone but there was a three-quarter moon, and we could see that almost all the Gray Gulls were gone by that time and the calls had ceased. At 2345 we heard a variety of Gray Gull calls and found a flock of at least 100 active birds along the beach, many of them feeding. At 0030 on 20 January we could hear many of them calling over the water and could see some in flight, and checks at 0400 and 0600 showed that several hundred were present. After daybreak there was a perceptible increase, and by 0800 there were many hundreds throughout the area. During the morning there were sequences of courtship activity and copulation, but this appeared not to be at high intensity. We have no way of knowing if some or all of these birds were from the Pampa del Miraje colony, but the fact that the departure and arrival times of the birds on the coast were about one hour offset from the peak arrival and departure times of birds in the desert makes that a reasonable inference. Certainly most Gray Gulls leave the coast at dusk; many then reappear there about two hours later and there is much activity and feeding all during the night, which is in accord with our inferences based on observations in the nesting colony. Presumably the movements between nesting colony and coast are similar after the eggs have hatched.

JUVENILES ON THE COAST

Our only information on the activities of juveniles on the coast comes from Adrian Brown, an experienced bird observer who resided for many years in Antofagasta and who often visited Mejillones, 60 km N of Antofagasta, where there are extensive sandy beaches frequented by Gray Gulls. Brown has kindly provided the following notes (edited for brevity):

28 March 1970. In early afternoon my attention was attracted by continuous squeaking cries of a young *Garuma* begging from an adult bird in a small group of adults. The adult bird gave no response and did not attempt to feed the young bird. The young one was light brown in color, with no signs of adult gray feathers and no white tips to the secondaries. In flight the tail showed a clearly defined chocolate-colored band. While under observation the young gull made no attempt to feed itself on the "sand fleas" *(Emerita analoga)* eaten by the adult birds. 1 and 3 May 1970, about 1600 hrs. There are several hundred *Garumas* scattered along the beach, of which about 20 percent are immatures. Adult birds are feeding on crustaceans by probing into the sand as the waves recede, but the young gulls make no attempt to do so. They are begging from adults without apparent success. The only feeding activity by the young is to peck at possibly edible material accumulated at the high-water mark along the beach. Some young birds were lighter brown than others, and the wings appeared more speckled; some had very dark primaries. I presume these differences correspond to different ages.

These observations indicate that young of the year were present on the coast 33 days after our departure from the Pampa del Miraje colony. Smith and Diem (1972) reported young *Larus californicus* as able to fly well by an age of about 48 days. Given the stage of development of many young birds in the nesting area of 23 February, the juvenile seen on 28 March might have come from the Miraje colony.

THE PAMPA IN THE NONBREEDING SEASON

On 21 August 1970 Araya and Millie revisited the site of the nesting colony in the Pampa del Miraje, arriving at 1900 and finding no gulls. Both observers were awake most of the night. At 2030 they heard calls of perhaps five or six gulls, apparently in flight, that persisted for about 30 minutes. No other gull sounds were heard for the rest of the night. At 0500 on 22 August they commenced a walk over all the main areas of the colony and did not see or hear a single gull. Although local residents in the nitrate mining communities mention hearing gulls at night at various times, there is presently no certain evidence that Gray Gulls other than a few wanderers visit or roost in the interior deserts at any time except during the breeding season.

DISCUSSION
ETHOLOGY

The literature on the behavior of gulls is enormous and still growing. A survey of the major ornithological and behavioral journals and monograph series over the past two decades shows an abundance of papers intensively analyzing the behavior of familiar species or providing detailed descriptions of the activities of previously little-known forms that nest in remote areas. In fact, this well-studied group of birds provides much of the data for contemporary ethological interpretations of avian display. Most of the basic displays and vocalizations of gulls are described, reviewed, and discussed by Tinbergen (1953, 1959) and Moynihan (1955a, 1955b, 1958a, 1958b, 1959a, 1962), and notable subsequent contributions dealing with additional species include studies of *L. bulleri* (Beer, 1965, 1966; Evans, 1970), *L. fuscus* (Brown, 1967), *L. hemprichi* (Fogden, 1964), *L. glaucescens* (Vermeer, 1963), *Creagrus furcatus* (Hailman, 1964; Nelson, 1968a, 1968b), and *Xema sabini* (Brown et al. 1967).

Even with this wealth of ethological information, the behavior of the Gray Gull merits particular attention. Its nesting habitat and some of its habits differ from those of every other gull species. Moynihan, who has studied intensively more species of larids than any other ethologist, singled out the Gray Gull as having "the most unspecialized, the most nearly primitive display repertoire of any gull whose behavior has been studied in detail.... [It] does not seem to have any display which is not found in the same or very similar form in many other species.... This would indicate that all its displays are comparatively old characters in the family Laridae" (1962:98). Using data from his 1962 paper, Moynihan (1970) cited *L. modestus* as one of the bird species with the greatest known number — 28 — of distinctive major displays, and this figure was subsequently cited by Wilson (1972) under the name White-hooded Gull in an article on animal communication. Moynihan cautioned that his figures for this and other species were "crude and approximate," and behavioral repertoires including greater numbers of displays will probably be revealed by close study. On the coast we noted one Gray Gull display — Rock-pulling or Pecking-into-the-ground — that was not recorded by Moynihan and which is also shown by many other gull species. We did not detect any additional major displays by adults on the nesting grounds.

Vocalizations are extremely important in the behavior of the Gray Gull, and the relevant literature on vocal communication in birds is truly overwhelming. We will not attempt to cite more than a few of many significant contributions. An appropriate first reference in this field is the pioneer study of Craig (1908) on the uses of vocalizations in pigeons (Columbidae). Implicit in Craig's study is the concept that the same vocalization may evoke different results depending on the context in which it is used, and many subsequent authors have more explicitly stressed this (Collias, 1960). Smith (1963, 1965, 1969) has discussed the message, meaning, and context of avian vocalizations in detail, and his analysis seems especially relevant to Gray Gull behavior. He suggested (1969) that each display communicates a set of messages or information of somewhat general nature, and that more specific information may be provided largely by the context in which the display is given. For example, every display inherently includes at least some information about the category to which the displayer belongs (as described by Craig) and also information about the probability of some action(s) by the displayer. The circumstances under which the display is given may specify the probability or predictability of a particular action. Of course, some displays are more specific than others and may signal more precise messages in addition to generalized and contextual information.

Gull behavior has been intensively analyzed from the standpoint of possible motivations or drives, of interspecific homologies, and in terms of the possible precise information communicated by displays, but there has been much less analysis along the lines suggested by Smith. We have therefore examined some major displays of the Gray Gull and attempted to identify first the more general and then the more specific behavioral information that they encode.

Ethologists sometimes purposely use anthropomorphic phrases to describe the apparent information content of behavior patterns. This procedure often saves many words, and for that reason we will use a few "quotations" to indicate our interpretation of displays. We do not intend, of course, any suggestion that the bird conceptualizes in such a manner.

We chose for analysis the Long Call, Choking, the Low Oblique-Mew Call, Head-tossing, and the Hunched Posture as these are frequent and conspicuous displays and are also found in all other species of gulls that have been studied. In discussing these displays one should keep in mind the following facts about gulls in general and the Gray Gull in particular. (1) The postures used in silent displays are often similar or identical among many species, but displays accompanied by vocalizations are more likely to be posturally distinctive and the vocalizations themselves are usually species-specific. (2) To the human observer, at least, the sexes are identical in external appearance except that females average slightly smaller than males. Evidently the male is always the larger bird in any pair, but some females are larger than some males and behavioral cues must be important in learning the sex of an individual. (3) Apart from activities such as copulation and courtship feeding in which the role of the sexes necessarily differs, there are no sexual differences in displays and vocalizations. (4) During the important nocturnal activities of the Gray Gull in the nesting colony, slight size differences or subtle visual signals are probably not detectable except at very close range. Therefore, mate recognition at night may involve not only contextual information such as territory or nest site location but probably individual differences in vocalization.

The Long Call (pls. 16, 17) is most often given within a bird's territory, especially the nesting territory, and in response to the approach of another bird either in flight or on foot. Moynihan's impression that "Long Calls of the Gray Gull are comparatively rare" (1962:74) was gained entirely from daytime observation on the coast, where territories are temporary and shifting. In the nesting colony, Long Calls are one of the most frequently heard components of the nocturnal chorus, although seldom heard during the day when activity is much reduced. Gray Gulls sometimes give Long Calls seemingly without any specific stimulus, but a bird may be reacting to signals that are not readily apparent to the human observer and the call is never given when there is no activity of other birds in the vicinity. It may be given by a bird actively establishing a territory or by one that is otherwise quietly incubating eggs or brooding chicks. An approaching bird often gives a Long Call in response to that of the approached bird, whether or not they are mates or of the same sex, and the presence or activity of a small chick may elicit a Long Call from an adult. The general message of the Long Call seems to be to establish the calling bird's location and indicate a state of readiness to interact. It is a typical advertisement, in which the bird in effect proclaims "I am here! Notice me!" Among rival males, this proclamation may carry a threat of attack; among potential mates, it may be a signal in establishing a pair bond and may later become part of a greeting ceremony. Depending on the context, the Long Call may signify that the bird is on its (claimed) territory and that an approaching adult bird should "identify" itself. We have no evidence that Gray Gull chicks respond specifically to this call although it may make them notice an adult's presence; chicks did not consistently approach or retreat when it was given. As previously suggested, the frequent exchange of Long Calls by nesting birds at night may serve to facilitate individual recognition although the Mew Call may be more important in this respect (see below). Our impression is that the Long Call does not inherently indicate more than the general behavioral message of readiness to interact; subsequent actions depend on the response of the other bird. This view is consistent with the use of this call by other gull species in association with a variety of situations (Beer, 1970b).

In the Gray Gull, the movements associated with Choking (pl. 19) are so similar to nest-scrape–making that it seems certain that the display is a ritualized form of that activity. Other suggested sources of Choking are regurgitation and placing of nest material (Tinbergen, 1959), but the Gray Gull never uses nest material in any manner and the retching movements of the foreparts are not as pronounced as they are in the Choking of some other species. Choking is usually accompanied by a series of muffled yelps with the bill opened slightly but sometimes the Mew Call is given. This display usually occurs in potential conflict situations associated with nesting territories, and a frequent pattern is for a bird (A) on its territory to charge toward another (B) near the boundary of the territory. Bird B starts Choking and is not attacked; instead, Bird A also goes into Choking. The general message seems to be "I am within my territory; I am ready to attack if you intrude." If the birds are both males, Bird B's Choking may signal, "I will fight if you attack" (Tinbergen, 1959). Bird A's Choking indicates recognition of this, gives the same message, and thereby defines the edge of his nesting territory. If Bird B is a female and recognized as such by male Bird A, this changes the context and A may then respond to B as a potential mate that may nest within his territory. The general message applies in both cases, but the information provided by Choking is augmented by recognition of the sex of each bird. As this is a display usually performed right beside another bird, the chance of distinguishing at least the sex and possibly the individual is maximized. We subsequently suggest that the Mew Call is used for individual recognition, and the sometime use of the Mew Call during Choking is consistent with this possibility. Choking may also be given by a lone bird on its territory with no others close by, or in response to activities of a chick (p. 26). In the first instance the display is probably a signal of territoriality to a potential intruder. In the second, the adult may be expressing its territoriality and redirecting an aggressive drive toward a chick just as it does with a mate.

In the Gray Gull Choking is rarely seen on the coast but is often shown by birds in the nesting colony, which indicates close association of this display with nesting sites and activities. If Choking is derived from nest-making behavior and symbolizes this, it constitutes a source of information that may be augmented in different ways according to the circumstances in which the display is given. It can serve to prevent destructive territorial fights between rivals and also to blunt aggressive drives between mates—more rarely, between adult and chick. Hence, Choking may function as either "aggressive" or "friendly," depending on the context in which it is used.

The Low Oblique Posture (pl. 18) and the Mew Call are not always associated together, but if any vocalization is given with the Low Oblique it is the Mew Call. Beer (1970b) uses the term Crooning to describe this vocalization in *L. atricilla*, in order to avoid implications of homology with some other calls that have been called "Mew." We have no data bearing on this question, but what we term the Mew Call for consistency is clearly the same as what Beer calls Crooning, and Croon is certainly a better phonetic description of the Gray Gull's prolonged note of changing pitch.

The Low Oblique–Mew Call is usually given during an interaction with a (potential) mate or chick, sometimes just before disgorging food as in courtship feeding or in feeding the young. Beer (1969, 1970a) and Evans (1970) demonstrated that chicks of *L. atricilla* (6 days old) and *L. bulleri* (3 to 4 days old) can distinguish the Mew Calls of their own parents from those of other adults and that this vocalization is used by parents to attract their chicks. In the Gray Gull, however, adults seldom direct the Mew Call to chicks and we did not find that parents call up their chicks with this or other vocalizations. We suggest that an important function of the Mew Call in *L. modestus* is to permit vocal recognition of individual adults. Beer (1972) found the Crooning Call of *L. atricilla* varied considerably between individual adults but also within the same individual, and he was unable to detect evidence of recognition among adults based on this call. Tinbergen (1953) believed that Herring Gull mates distinguished one another by their Mew Calls, basing this on field observation. Evans (1970) showed by sound spectrograms that the Mew Calls of *L. bulleri* differ individually and consistently, but he did not test for recognition between adults. Our field data strongly suggest to us that Gray Gull adults use the Mew Call for individual recognition.

On the coast and in the nesting colony in the pre-egg stage two Gray Gulls often make long, parallel Low Oblique runs that culminate in Mew Calls. Our observations and those of Moynihan indicate that these birds are usually potential mates, and if so or even if not, the Mew Calling may be part of a process of learning to recognize individuals. The frequent use of Low Oblique–Mew Calls by birds seeking their mates on the nests at night may be a means of communicating individual identity, and this display pattern is particularly prevalent among courting birds at night. As the Gray Gull probably cannot depend on visual recognition in the dark, there would be a great advantage in having individually recognizable vocal signals. The message of this call may be generally to signal individual identity that may then be specifically recognizable as that of a mate or parent, or as neither. The bird receiving this information may then respond accordingly, with aggression sometimes resulting when nonmates are involved. The use of the Mew Call during Choking presumably has the same function of individual recognition—either as a (potential) rival or mate, possibly as a parent. As Gray Gull chicks will seek and often receive shelter and food from adults other than their parents and as this behavior appears to facilitate chick survival, emphasis on individual recognition at this stage could be disadvantageous and the sparing use of the Mew Call in parent-chick interactions is understandable.

The Low Oblique Posture, with or without vocalization, is used in feeding chicks, in courtship feeding, and in approaches of one bird to another that may develop into either hostile or sexual behavior. This great variety of contexts makes it difficult to identify a common general message for the Low Oblique. It may be an obligatory posture for regurgitating large amounts of food, which suggests that its derivational history is from feeding chicks to courtship feeding of adults to ritualization as an adult display with no feeding. To chicks it is associated with feeding and thus connotes nonaggression and probably bond-establishment, even if temporary as when chicks are fed by a foster parent. Adult males use this posture in feeding adult females, and the females often approach males in a Hunched Posture that changes to a Low Oblique. The Hunched appears to be a nonaggressive posture (see below), and in these contexts the Low Oblique seems associated with nonattack and bond-formation. A bird sometimes approaches another in a Low Oblique Posture, however, and aggressive action follows. We suggest that the posture does not signal aggression but nonaggression, and that agonistic behavior results only if prompted by the response of the approached bird, whose displays or vocalizations indicate that it is not a (potential) mate and that conflict with the approacher is imminent. Moynihan noted that Low Oblique–Mew Call patterns were especially associated with pairing (1962:83-84), but also commented that "they are rather frequently associated with overt attack (Table II)." Table II lists only seven specific observations of Low Obliques with Mew Calls, and only two of these were associated with attacks. We feel that our suggested interpretation of the Gray Gull's Low Oblique–Mew Call as a generally nonaggressive, individual recognition, bond-establishing display is consistent with the available data.

The Head-toss is always accompanied by a soft note ("Kioo" of Moynihan) which has a juvenile sound. In the following, we discuss Head-tossing with the understanding that the note is always given with it. The general message communicated by the Head-toss appears to be solicitation. A solicitation is an attempt to get another individual to yield something of value without fighting, particularly something that cannot be obtained by fighting but only through the other's cooperation. The Head-toss almost always precedes courtship feeding and copulation, which have in common the fact that they will take place only with the cooperation of the solicited individual and cannot be brought about by force. More specific messages are given by nibbling at the male's bill by the female—specifying courtship feeding—and by Head-tossing by both sexes, which always precedes copulation attempts. This display may be derived from the feeding solicitations of young birds (Tinbergen, 1959) for the posture is similar and the juvenile-sounding note suggests a relationship. Moynihan (1959a) described begging with Head-tossing and the Kioo Note in 12- to 14-day-old chicks of *L. pipixcan* and *L. delewarensis*.

Moynihan recorded Head-tossing by adult Gray Gulls following a Long Call, and also during attack and escape runs by immature birds. The first case may be interpreted as generalized solicitation following an advertisement of the bird's presence. The second case is puzzling but may be attributable to immaturity. Young birds usually rush toward a parent and give Head-tosses soliciting feeding, and they may give Head-tosses while retreating from an aggressive adult; this juvenile pattern of interaction with other individuals may persist for some time even if no longer appropriate, as in a hostile situation.

The Hunched Posture is not accompanied by a vocalization, and its general message appears to be that of nonaggressiveness. In the Gray Gull we often noted a moderate Hunched Posture (pl. 8) in which the neck is retracted but the head is only slightly lowered. This posture is the one most frequently assumed by birds returning to their nests at night, and this or the definitive Hunched Posture (pl. 20) was also used by birds in the daytime as they threaded their way to their own nests through the territories of others without prompting attacks. In popular contemporary parlance, these birds need a "low profile" and assume it quite literally when a state of nonaggression is to be signaled. The frequent use of the Hunched Posture by soliciting birds—especially initially—is consistent with this view.

These interpretations are deliberately simplistic, for we have sought to identify the simplest common denominator of each display in a species that appears to have the broadest and least specialized range of displays of all the larids. Like morphological and physiological characters, behavior patterns undoubtedly evolve in response to selective pressures in different situations and even the "common denominators" of displays found throughout the genus *Larus* or the family Laridae may have changed among the various species. Our suggestions are based entirely on observations of the Gray Gull, and may or may not be applicable to other species. There are no clear-cut nonbehavioral reasons for supposing the Gray Gull to be primitive, and the absence of more complex specializations in its displays may be related to its seminocturnality during the breeding season. On balance, selection has probably not favored the evolution or retention of distinctive visual and postural signals that are of little or no use in the dark and without any similar species nesting close by. The Gray Gull's displays may be primarily or secondarily unspecialized, and in either case we propose our simplistic interpretations as a possible base line to which the usually more elaborate behavior patterns of other species may be compared.

A Behavioral Analogy

After many hours of studying gulls in the field and behavioral literature in the library, one of us (Howell) offers a modest proposal as an aid to interpreting gull behavior. I suggest that it is similar to the game of chess and that displays are like chess pieces. In the following account, the pieces and their moves are interchangeable with displays and their use. Each piece symbolizes a finite number of possible actions, and this is recognized by all players of the game. The use of a certain piece may signify attack, defense, threat, bluff, diversion, or retreat to a stronger position, depending on the context. Other pieces are of less varied significance, and their use may be associated with rather specific situations. At times, almost any piece may be moved as a "throwaway" gesture, indicative of conflicting drives and an impulse to do something even if inappropriate for the situation at hand.

Pieces that can move in many possible directions command attention whenever they are used, and the same is true of pieces with more restricted options but high predictability of action. Other pieces are relatively weak and are usually used tentatively, as a prelude to a subsequent more pronounced action.

Although the number of different pieces is small and their possible actions are limited, their use in different contexts introduces considerable variety into the game. Even though players recognize the pieces and their symbolism, one player is never completely certain of another's complex motivational state and will respond, presumably, to the most probable information signified by the use of a given piece. Sometimes there is ambiguity and confusion—Player A moves a piece for defense, but Player B responds as though to a threat. In any case, B's response probably determines A's next move, and A's then determines B's next. A player, however, may at times proceed with a ritualized, predetermined pattern of moves which is carried to completion regardless of the other's responses.

The analogy cannot be carried much further. Among gulls, after a few exchanges of pieces or perhaps an exchange of more subtle signals, the players may become partners instead of opponents. If they remain opponents, it is likely that each will settle for a secure stalemate instead of attempting to sweep one another from the board.

The "general message" of the analogy is that it is risky, both for participants and observers, to assume with too much confidence a knowledge of the motivational states behind the displays.

DESERT NESTING: ADVANTAGES AND ADAPTATIONS

The Gray Gull's exclusive use of barren inland desert areas for nesting is extraordinary and unique. Many other species of gulls nest inland but around lakes and marshes; many gulls and other seabirds nest in arid terrestrial habitats but only when these are islands, with water and food close by. The only important advantage to nesting in an extreme desert is freedom from predation. Freedom from competition for nest sites is also a benefit, but this follows from the lack of predation as that removes most of the advantage of securing particular sites. We have mentioned four possible predators (other than man) in the desert nesting colony, none of which seems very important. Each of these is more abundant along the coast, and other potential predators also appear there. We suggest that the critical predator along the coast and on the coastal islands is the Kelp Gull, a large, aggressive species that clearly dominates *L. modestus* whenever they meet. *L. dominicanus* is similar in appearance and habits to the black-backed gulls *(L. marinus* and *L. fuscus)* of the northern hemisphere and is highly predatory in nesting colonies (Murphy, 1936). Successful nesting by *L. modestus* may require the absence of *L. dominicanus,* and as the latter is present all along the coast and offshore islands, the Gray Gulls must nest inland. The devastating effect of predation by large gulls on smaller ones has been documented in other species. For example, Kruuk (1964) cites a case in which a centuries-old colony of thousands of pairs of *L. ridibundus* on Walney Island in the Irish Sea was totally eliminated within 30 years after Herring Gulls and Lesser Black-backed Gulls arrived and began nesting on the island.

The potential disadvantages of nesting in the desert include the severe climate, the need for long commuting flights and long attentive periods, and presumably the need to rear the young to a sufficiently mature stage for them to fly to the coast. No nesting colony other than the one in the Pampa del Miraje has been studied, and we do not know if climatic conditions in other colonies are similar. In the Miraje colony we believe that the afternoon wind is critically important, for all ambient temperatures are still rising by the time the wind starts and heat stress might otherwise be too great for either eggs, chicks, or attending adults. Successful colony sites are possibly limited to areas where winds keep the heat below damaging levels, which may explain why nesting colonies are not more widely distributed than seems to be the case. As yet uninvestigated are the possible effects of the often extremely low humidity, particularly on eggs that are exposed to the dry air for several hours each day as the parent shades them.

One reason for believing the wind to be so important is the fact that we found no exceptional physiological adaptations to thermal stress beyond those found in other larids that inhabit less extreme habitats. Adaptations of adults to heat stress include responses such as evaporative cooling by panting, facing into the wind when it blows, ruffling out the plumage for maximum unloading of body heat and for insulation against solar radiation, and rock-standing with the feet in the shade. The possible importance of dark pigmentation is discussed subsequently. Under extreme heat stress in still air the smallest chicks die, slightly older ones seek what shade there is and pant, and the larger ones can maintain a safe body temperature by panting. When the wind blows, even the smaller chicks can thermoregulate in full sun with the help of evaporative cooling.

We regard the nonpredatory behavior of Gray Gulls toward their own eggs and chicks as an adaptation that favors reproductive success in their unique breeding habitat. Among many other species of gulls, predation on the eggs and chicks of their own and other gull species in the nesting area is an important source of mortality, as exemplified by a mixed colony of *L. californicus* and *L. delawarensis* studied by Vermeer (1970). The Gray Gull has no neighboring congeners or any other species of nesting birds on which to prey, but despite many opportunities afforded for conspecific predation when we flushed large numbers of nesting gulls, we never saw an intact egg or a chick eaten. Such upflights occurred each time we entered or left a blind, and we would surely have seen at least one instance of egg or chick predation by returning birds if this were a regular part of the species' behavioral repertoire. As the nesting colonies of the Gray Gull are isolated from those of all other birds, a loss of the tendency to eat eggs and chicks would only reduce self-predation and would not reduce energy gain at the expense of other species. This nonpredation is probably a derived condition as most other gulls are strongly predaceous on eggs and chicks. Furthermore, adult Gray Gulls are still agonistic toward chicks (including their own) that are out of the nest, but they usually stop short of fatal attacks in response to the Beak-hiding appeasement posture of the chicks. The acceptance by adults of any chick once it gets under the adult bird may be symptomatic of the apparent intraspecific reduction of predatory behavior of adults toward offspring.

Whatever the cause, the behavior of adults in accepting any chicks seems certain to increase chances of survival of offspring in general. Gray Gull chicks, like those of other species, begin to wander from the nest scrape within a few days of age at most. Unlike those of many other species they are thereby exposed to potentially damaging or fatal heat stress unless able to find shelter, and in the desert there is virtually no shelter except under an adult. Two options are open that lead to maximum survival—either the chicks must not wander or must return quickly to their own scrape as ambient temperatures soar, or adults must not discriminate among those chicks that they will attend once the chicks are under them. The second strategy seems to be operative. The "logical" anthropomorphic solution would be for chicks to remain in their own nest scrape—there is nothing to be gained by wandering in the desert—or for adults to go to their own chicks and shade them if they do leave the scrape, but neither of these things happens.

Roberts (1900) wrote a somewhat incredible account of parent-chick relationships in *L. pipixcan*, part of which was quoted in A. C. Bent's *Life Histories of North American Gulls and Terns* (1921; reprinted 1947). Roberts reported that when young chicks of this marsh-nesting species swam away from their nests and were carried by wind toward dangerous open water, adults repeatedly picked them up and flung them back toward the nesting area where they often scrambled into the nearest nest. He described the chicks as "exhausted and bleeding" from this treatment, and one must doubt if Roberts correctly interpreted this as a rescue operation instead of a case of adults attacking or preying on stray chicks. Whichever the case, there is no reason to question Roberts' account of many chicks being accepted by any adult into whose nest they might clamber, with some adults attending as many as 12 chicks in the same nest. This situation is basically similar to that seen in the Gray Gull colony, that is, wandering chicks are exposed to extreme environmental hazards and chances of survival of the greatest number are enhanced by any adult's acceptance of any chick that gets into its nest.

The high degree of nocturnal activity in the nesting colony is advantageous as many hours during the day are too hot for more than simple maintenance behavior and as the distance from nest to feeding grounds would make frequent shuttling between coast and colony energetically extravagant. This may be too simple an explanation, however, for the presence of a diffuse reflective layer in the eye suggests a long-term adaptation to nocturnality. As almost all gulls are largely diurnal in their breeding activities we presume that the seminocturnal habits of *L. modestus* during the breeding season represent a derived condition, but we have no evidence on how this may have originated.

The relatively long incubation period and small clutch size as compared with other gulls of similar size exemplifies convergence toward other seabirds that must go long distances from the nesting area to feed. In the virtual absence of predation, ability to provide shelter and food for the young seems to be the only ultimately important factor mitigating against the more usual *Larus* clutch of three eggs. The fact that the incubation patch is reduced to a two-part structure suggests genetically linked control of patch shape and of clutch size, but so little is known of the factors that determine size and shape of the incubation patch that any such suggestion is highly speculative. In any case, the low clutch size in association with the need to travel long distances from the nest for food is consistent with Lack's (1967) hypotheses on small clutches in offshore-feeding marine birds.

Despite their relative freedom from predation on the nesting grounds, Gray Gulls are wary there (especially at night) and fly up in alarm at any disturbance, even the silent beam of a flashlight. We have so far not considered man as one of the potential predators, but this may not be justified. In recent years, as Johnson pointed out, many thousands of Gray Gull eggs have been taken by modern man. The Miraje colony itself is crossed by still detectable foot trails of ancient Indian tribes that traveled from the interior to the coast in search of food and salt. Primitive man existed in this part of South America for thousands of years before historic times, and it is possible that man preyed on gull colonies (if they existed then) for a large part of the post-Pleistocene era—but this, too, is pure speculation.

TAXONOMIC RELATIONSHIPS

The Gray Gull has been considered closely related to *L. heermanni* and *L. fuliginosus* at least since Ridgway (1919) placed these three species and *belcheri* in the genus *Blasipus*. Although *modestus* and *heermanni* are highly colonial, *fuliginosus* is a solitary nester. *L. modestus* and *heermanni* are very similar in external appearance as they are gray with a white head, but *L. modestus* is smaller and has a more slender bill. *L. fuliginosus* differs from these two as it is gray with a black head (see Bailey, 1961, 1962 for photographs). The only detailed published data on displays of *fuliginosus* are those of Moynihan (1962) and Nelson (1968b). There are no detailed published accounts of the displays of *L. heermanni*, but Howell visited the principal breeding colony of this species on Isla Raza, Baja California, Mexico, in March 1972 and took extensive notes, tape recordings, and motion pictures. The displays of the three species seem to be quite different. Moynihan states that the Long Call of *fuliginosus* is given from an Oblique to Low Oblique Posture, and this is confirmed by Nelson's description of the Long Call as given "with head and neck held low and parallel to the ground." This posture is almost the reverse of that of *modestus* or *heermanni*, which raise the head vertically during the same call. The postural changes accompanying the Long Call of *heermanni* are like those of many other *Larus* species (but not *modestus* or *fuliginosus*) in that the head is first bowed so that the bill points between the feet, then two muffled notes are given with the head down, and then a series of about seven "Kaks" of diminishing amplitude as the head is thrown upward to a vertical position. Sometimes up to 15 Kaks are given. As the call starts, the carpal joints are conspicuously abducted, much more so than in *modestus*. As mentioned, *modestus* does not lower the head but begins the Long Call with the head horizontal and raises it to vertical. The only other postures of *fuliginosus* described by Moynihan and Nelson—

Hunched, Uprights, Bill-downs ("Foot-looking," pl. 17) seem the same as those of most other gulls. *L. heermanni* differs from *modestus* not only in the Long Call but in several other displays. The Mew Call is more of a bray than a moan or croon, and is usually given from a horizontal Oblique rather than a Low Oblique, and the bill is widely open. Choking is usually much more pronounced, with vigorous pumping movements and wide-open bill, and also varies from a standing to a crouching position. The Head-toss Note sounds like a much-amplified "wheep" note of a juvenile bird, not like the Kioo of *modestus,* and the Copulation Call of the male is a loud "Kak-kak-kak, etc." unlike the muffled call of *modestus*. Surprisingly, no Hunched Postures were seen. Howell's observations on *heermanni* were all made during the pre-egg stage, but birds were paired and sitting on nest scrapes. All had at least some materials worked into the scrapes, either pieces of vegetation or good-sized feathers, and he often saw birds picking up and carrying old molted feathers to their nest scrapes. As the gull population is huge and some parts of the island are devoid of vegetation some nests may be simple scrapes in the sand, but the birds seem to use nest material if any at all is available. The few nests of *fuliginosus* described to date have included pieces of driftwood (Bailey, 1961, 1962). In contrast, *modestus* never uses nest material of any kind although old feathers, weathered bones, and small pebbles are plentiful.

In summary, although *modestus* and *heermanni* are very similar in color pattern and probably more closely related to each other than to any other *Larus* species, they are behaviorally quite distinct. *L. fuliginosus* is very different, and we agree with Moynihan (1959b) that *fuliginosus* is not closely related to the two white-hooded gulls *(modestus* and *heermanni)* but is closest to some of the other dark-hooded gulls such as *L. atricilla.* In fact, *fuliginosus* superficially resembles a large "melanistic" counterpart of the *atricilla* type in which virtually all the white areas, including neck, body, tail, and tips of the inner primaries and secondaries have become gray. Only the feathers of the eyelids are white, forming a conspicuous contrasting mark as in most dark-hooded gulls.

Plumage Color

Writing about *L. fuliginosus,* Hailman (1963) asked "Why is the Lava Gull the color of lava?" His answer was that cryptic coloration was not needed by adults to avoid predation as they have essentially no predators, but that gray color helps them avoid detection by piratic Frigate Birds *(Fregata magnificens)* while the gulls scavenge on dark lava-sand beaches. Adult Gray Gulls have few predators but are harassed on the coast by the Kelp Gull and Band-tailed Gull. These three species are usually found together along the coast, often foraging or resting side by side, so we doubt that the gray color of *modestus* functions importantly in avoiding detection and harassment by the larger species. The Gray Gull matches well the color of the substrate in its nesting area, but concealing coloration can be of little or no selective value as adult gulls have virtually no predators while on the ground and as the colony is extremely conspicuous because of upflights at any disturbance during the day and the high noise level at night. Either on the coast or in the nesting colony, crypsis seems to offer only slight selective advantage at best and alternative explanations should be considered.

Tinbergen (1964) cites evidence from Phillips (1962) that gull models with white underparts were less alarming to subsurface fishes than models that were dark ventrally, indicating that white underparts provide an advantage in foraging over water. Cowan (1972) reviewed the subject and criticized these conclusions. An obvious criticism is that many species of gulls are darkly mottled during their first year of life—a particularly critical period if they are to survive to reproductive age and thus a poor time to be at a disadvantage in foraging. The fact that all but a few species of gulls have dark mantles and white underparts as adults is strong presumptive evidence of some advantage to that condition and perhaps an advantage in foraging is one of several, including use as a social signal (Armstrong, 1971). Whatever the possible advantages, the few exceptions to the typical gull color pattern—those that are entirely dark ventrally as adults—merit particular attention.

The only gull species with completely dark underparts as adults are *L. heermanni*, *L. fuliginosus*, and *L. modestus*. *Larus (Leucophaeus; Gabianus) scoresbii* of sub-Antarctic South America is light pearl gray ventrally. *L. hemprichi* and *L. leucophthalmus*, which breed in arid tropical areas along the coasts of east Africa, the Red Sea, and the Gulf of Aden, have dark heads and blackish mantles and gray breasts but white abdomens. Thus, with the exception of *scoresbii*, the most extensively dark gulls nest in arid terrain in hot climates and are exposed to intense solar radiation during the breeding season. Of the three darkest forms, *heermanni* nests in greatest numbers at about latitude 28° N on desert islands in the Gulf of California that have high daytime temperatures and almost no shade that is usable by adult gulls. *Fuliginosus* and *modestus* nest within the tropics in virtually unshaded and barren habitats. The correlation between mostly dark pigmentation and nesting areas exposed to intense solar radiation suggests that extensive melanization of the plumage may be an adaptation to that environmental condition, but all possible advantages of the largely gray coloration of these gulls should be considered.

The principal possible advantages would seem to be concealment from predators or prey, protection against excess plumage abrasion, protection against ultraviolet radiation, and thermoregulation.

Concealment from predators is unlikely to be important as the birds are either very conspicuous through their activity in the nesting colonies *(heermanni, modestus)* or they have no important predators as adults. Concealment from piratic Frigate Birds may be a real advantage to *fuliginosus* as Hailman (1963) proposed but would not apply to the other two species. Concealment from prey is also unlikely, and according to the Phillips and Tinbergen hypothesis these species should be more conspicuous to swimming prey than gulls that are white ventrally. Possibly the feeding habits of the grayer gulls require less concealment. *L. modestus* frequently feeds by probing for *Emerita* in the sand, and it forages in the Humboldt Current where marine life is often superabundant. *L. heermanni* also feeds occasionally by sand-probing and nests in areas where the offshore marine fauna may be very abundant. *L. fuliginosus* may also probe for food and depends heavily on scavenging (Snow and Snow, 1969).

Heavy melanin deposition in feathers apparently increases resistance to abrasion, as is evident in black wing tips (Averill, 1923), but there is no indication that the grayer gulls are subject to greater abrasive forces than are other species. The winds in the Pampa del Miraje carry powdery dust but we did not experience any sandstorms or sand-blasting effects.

Melanin absorbs wavelengths in the ultraviolet range and can protect against penetration of excessive and potentially damaging radiation to the skin or deeper tissues. All adult gulls except a few Arctic or sub-Arctic nesters have gray or blackish mantles and wings, and this pigmentation may provide some protection from excessive ultraviolet radiation for species that nest in the open. There is little exposure of the ventral surface to such radiation, however, and if ultraviolet radiation were a serious problem, one might also expect that low-latitude high-altitude nesters such as the Andean Gull *(L. serranus)* would have the most saturated pigmentation, but this is not so.

If the more extensive melanin pigmentation of the species under discussion does not have as sole or principal advantages crypsis, resistance to abrasion, or protection from ultraviolet radiation, the hot climates of their breeding ranges suggest that thermoregulation may be an important consideration. At first this seems unlikely as melanin absorbs rather than reflects much solar energy and might therefore increase the heat load of nesting birds in the sun. Absorption of solar heat at or near the outer surface of the plumage could prevent excessive heat-loading, though, if most of the heat could be dissipated without reaching the skin and deeper tissues. Unpigmented (white) feathers reflect visible light but may permit deeper penetration of other ranges of solar energy. The problem of optimal protection against solar heat has often been invoked to account for the fact that some desert-dwelling human tribes wear dark-colored clothing. Siple (1949) expressed the basis for this view that such clothing is well suited for protection against solar heat. "The dark color of the robe is probably more effective for keeping the radiant temperatures reduced than a translucent white one would be. This is based on the assumption that the opaque dark color causes absorption of radiation at the surface. This makes the surface abnormally hot and causes the dissemination of the heat by reradiation to the sky or to other bodies of lower temperature."

Experimental and theoretical support for this hypothesis is provided by studies on heat loading in Australian livestock. Macfarlane et al. (1956) found that Merino sheep exposed to high ambient temperatures in full sun maintained a skin temperature of 42°C while the temperature of the outer surface of the 4 cm–thick fleece rose to 87°C. The dark, weathered wool-tips absorbed more heat than paler fleece exposed by shearing, and shorn sheep with 1 cm–thick wool had skin temperatures 3°C higher than unshorn sheep with dark-tipped fleece three to four times as thick. Air movement caused marked reduction in the fleece surface temperature (Macfarlane, 1957). Priestley (1957) showed that heat loss by convection and long-wave radiation increases with an increase in the temperature of the fleece surface over that of the surrounding air, and this provides an "automatic compensating mechanism" that counters the heat-loading effect imposed by solar radiation. With even a slight wind much heat is dissipated by forced convection, and in the absence of wind the buoyancy of air coming in contact with the hot fleece surface carries away some heat by free convection. Schleger (1962) found that in "red" cattle with darker and lighter coat color, "the only significant correlation between color and [body] temperature is negative, i.e., darker animals have the lower temperature—the opposite of the relationship which might be expected. . . ." Kovarik (1964) provided a mathematical model analyzing the relationship of absorption of radiation and the resulting heat flow. His analysis showed that

increasing absorptivity, apart from causing a higher rate of heat generation, also reduces the mean depth at which this heat generation takes place. The resulting heat flow is divided between the animal body and the surrounding air mass in such a proportion that the total thermal load on the animal reaches a maximum at some intermediate value of absorptance rather than for the extremely dark cover . . . for a sufficiently large value of thermal resistance of the proctective layer, an increase of density of pigmentation beyond a certain value results in a reduction of the thermal load.

We find these data and hypotheses consistent with the Gray Gull's pigmentation and its behavior in the nesting colony. In the cold early morning, when feathers are kept sleeked, absorption of solar heat close to the skin would be advantageous. As the solar heat load increases, feathers are ruffled out to the maximum distance from the skin both dorsally and ventrally (pl. 9), providing high thermal resistance. The birds stand over their nests in the late morning and early afternoon, and the dark ventral feathers would protect against deep penetration of reflected solar energy and reradiation from the hot surface of the ground. Once the afternoon wind starts, heat loss by convection from the feather surface would be rapid and continuous and would protect the skin and deeper tissues from overheating.

Convective cooling by the afternoon wind is critically important for the Gray Gull as mates relieve each other only at night and an adult bird must remain at the nest all during the day. The other "gray" species, *heermanni* and *fuliginosus*, may not be exposed to invariable winds on their nesting grounds but nest relief doubtless occurs as in other diurnal gulls. An adult relieved during the day can take wing and quickly dissipate its surface heat load in flight, or it may go to the nearby sea and lose heat from the feathers by alighting on the water for bathing or feeding (Fogden, 1964). The subject of dark pigmentation and its thermal significance in animals is reviewed most recently by Hamilton (1973), and further experiments on the adaptive value of heavy melanization are clearly needed.

ORIGIN OF DESERT NESTING

The evolution of the desert-nesting habits of the Gray Gull remains a matter of conjecture. One possibility is that the gulls wandered inland for roosting and eventually stayed to nest, but there is no sure evidence that the birds roost in the desert during the nonbreeding season. Another possibility is that the presently known nesting areas were reached by gradual stages of movement inland from the more predator-occupied coast. Still another suggestion is that some present-day desert regions represent the dry beds of Quaternary or early Recent lakes, for which there is some geologic evidence.

The nitrate deposits characteristic of the northern Chilean deserts were probably laid down in the late Tertiary, 3 to 5 million years ago, following drainage and evaporation of inland seas. We think it unlikely that the Gray Gull's nesting behavior originated that long ago, and the species itself may not yet have evolved. Dr. Charles Meyer, Professor of Geology, University of California, Berkeley, informs us, however, that he noted wave-cut benches of probable Pleistocene age at the edges of the pampa near María Elena, about 35 km NE of the Pampa del Miraje. He believes that the present pampa in this region was probably covered by a lake in the late Pleistocene. This is not too far back in time for the species *modestus* to have existed, and suggests the possibility that these gulls originally moved inland to nest around lake borders as many other species do in other regions. If so, this pattern may have persisted as the lake(s) disappeared, with the gulls depending more and more on commuting to the coast for food. This extra energy expenditure may have been compensated for by an increasing scarcity of predators as surface water became scarcer or too mineralized. Continuation of the drying trend to the present extreme would ultimately lead to the contemporary situation in which *modestus* nests in the barren desert. All of the above suggestions are entirely speculative, and unfortunately it is unlikely that data that could settle the question can ever be obtained.

SUMMARY

The Gray Gull *(Larus modestus)* is an abundant species along much of the Pacific coast of South America but the only known nesting sites are in the barren deserts of the interior of northern Chile. In the Province of Antofagasta we studied the Gray Gull's courtship behavior on the coast and its nesting in a desert colony 5.5 km^2 in extent, including 10,000 pairs, about 30 km from the coast. The gulls maintain transient courting territories on the coast, and courtship behavior is similar to that of many other *Larus* species. At sunset all Gray Gulls leave the coast for the interior, and large numbers return to the coast at dawn. Territoriality and courtship continue in the nesting colony, especially at night. The nest is a simple scrape in the substrate and no materials are gathered. The usual clutch size is two or one, very rarely three, and the average is 1.55. There is a two-part incubation patch. The incubation span of each parent is about 24 hours, and changeovers occur only at night. Eggs are attended at all times, but during the hottest midday periods the adult stands and shades the nest. Strong wind invariably starts in early afternoon and reduces ambient temperatures from dangerously high levels. Nonincubating adults stand on rocks, which are cooler than the ground, and with their feet in the bird's own shade. The incubation period is at least 29 days. Chicks are fed primarily at night by parents coming from the coast, but some food is retained and regurgitated during the day. Young chicks wander from their nests, and when exposed to high heat stress seek shade under any nearby adult. Adults attack chicks but rarely kill and never eat them, and they accept any chick that gets under them. Very young chicks may die of overheating in still air, but older chicks can thermoregulate by panting. When exposed to the afternoon wind, chicks of all ages can lose enough heat to avoid fatal heat stress even if unshaded. There are no important predators on the nesting grounds but chick mortality is high, presumably from prolonged exposure in still air and from starvation. Our stay in the nesting colony was not long enough to see departures of juveniles for the coast.

We discuss the displays and vocalizations of the Gray Gull and compare them with those of other gulls, especially *L. heermanni* and *L. fuliginosus* which are also largely gray. We suggest that dark pigmentation of feathers may aid in avoiding excessive heat loading from solar radiation by allowing the outer surface to absorb heat and then lose it by convection, thus preventing deep penetration of heat to the body proper. In conclusion, we discuss the possible advantages and the possible historical origin of desert nesting in this species.

LITERATURE CITED

ARMSTRONG, E. A.
  1971. Social signalling and white plumage. Ibis 113:534.
AVERILL, C. K.
  1923. Black wing tips. Condor 25:57-59.
BAILEY, A. M.
  1961. Dusky and Swallow-tailed Gulls of the Galapagos Islands. Denver Mus. Nat. Hist. Pictorial 15:1-31.
  1962. Nesting of the Galapagos Penguin and the Galapagos Sooty Gull. Condor 64:159-161.
BARTH, E. K.
  1955. Egg-laying, incubation and hatching of the Common Gull *(Larus canus)*. Ibis 97: 222-239.
BEER, C. G.
  1965. Clutch size and incubation behavior in Black-billed Gulls *(Larus bulleri)*. Auk 82:1-18.
  1966. Adaptations to nesting habitat in the reproductive behavior of the Black-billed Gull *Larus bulleri*. Ibis 108:394-410.
  1969. Laughing Gull chicks: Recognition of their parents' voices. Science 166:1030-1032.
  1970a. On the responses of Laughing Gull chicks *(Larus atricilla)* to the calls of adults. I. Recognition of the voices of the parents. Anim. Behav. 18:652-660.
  1970b. On the responses of Laughing Gull chicks *(Larus atricilla)* to the calls of adults. II. Age changes and responses to different types of call. Anim. Behav. 18:661-677.
  1972. Individual recognition of voice and development in birds. Proc. XV Internat. Orn. Congr. Pp. 339-356.
BENT, A. C.
  1921. Life histories of North American gulls and terns. U. S. Nat. Mus. Bull. 113.
BROWN, R. G. B.
  1967. Courtship behaviour in the Lesser Black-backed Gull, *Larus fuscus*. Behaviour 29:122-153.
BROWN, R. B. G., N. G. BLURTON JONES, and D. J. T. HUSSELL.
  1967. The breeding behaviour of Sabine's Gull, *Xema sabini*. Behaviour 28:110-140.
CHAPMAN, S. E.
  1973. The Grey Gull. Sea Swallow 22:7-10.
COLLIAS, N. E.
  1960. An ecological and functional classification of animal sounds. *In:* Animal sounds and communication, ed. W. E. Lanyon and W. N. Tavolga. Amer. Inst. Biol. Sci. Publ. 7.
COWAN, P. J.
  1972. The contrast and coloration of sea birds: An experimental approach. Ibis 114: 390-393.
CRAIG, W.
  1908. The voices of pigeons regarded as a means of social control. Amer. J. Sociol. 14:86-100.
CULLEN, E.
  1957. Adaptations in the Kittiwake to cliff-nesting. Ibis 99:275-302.
DRENT, R.
  1967. Functional aspects of incubation in the Herring Gull (*Larus argentatus* Pont.). Leiden, E. J. Brill.
EVANS, R. M.
  1970. Parental recognition and the "mew call" in Black-billed Gulls *(Larus bulleri)*. Auk 87:503-513.
FOGDEN, M. P. L.
  1964. The reproductive behaviour and taxonomy of Hemprich's Gull *Larus hemprichi*. Ibis 106:299-320.

GOODALL, J. D., A. W. JOHNSON, and R. A. PHILIPPI
    1951. Las aves de Chile. Vol. II. Platt Establ. Gráficos, Buenos Aires.

GOODALL, J. D., R. A. PHILIPPI, and A. W. JOHNSON
    1945. Nesting habits of the Peruvian Gray Gull. Auk 62:450-451.

HAILMAN, J. P.
    1963. Why is the Galápagos Lava Gull the color of lava? Condor 65:528.
    1964. The Galápagos Swallow-tailed Gull is nocturnal. Wilson Bull. 76:347-354.

HAMILTON, W. J., III
    1973. Life's color code. New York, McGraw-Hill.

HARRIS, M. P.
    1964. Aspects of the breeding biology of the gulls *Larus argentatus*, *L. fuscus* and *L. marinus*. Ibis 106:432-456.

JOHNSON, A. W.
    1967. The birds of Chile and adjacent regions of Argentina, Bolivia and Peru. Vol. II. Platt Establ. Gráficos, Buenos Aires.

KOVARIK, M.
    1964. Flow of heat in an irradiated protective cover. Nature 201:1085-1087.

KRUUK, H.
    1964. Predators and anti-predator behaviour of the Black-headed Gull *(Larus ridibundus L.)*. Behaviour Suppl. XI:1-130.

LACK, D.
    1967. Interrelationships in breeding adaptations as shown by marine birds. Proc. XIV Internat. Orn. Congr. Pp. 3-42.

MACFARLANE, W. V.
    1957. Water economy and heat tolerance of tropical Merino sheep. *In:* Austral. Acad. Sci. Symp. on man and animals in the tropics. Brisbane, Univ. Queensland.

MACFARLANE, W. V., R. J. MORRIS, and B. HOWARD
    1956. Water economy of tropical Merino sheep. Nature 178:304-305.

MAUNDER, J. E., and W. THRELFALL
    1972. The breeding biology of the Black-legged Kittiwake in Newfoundland. Auk 89:789-816.

MOFFETT, G. M., JR.
    1969. The garuma—gull of the desert. Sea Frontiers 15:330-338.

MOYNIHAN, M.
    1955a. Some aspects of reproductive behaviour in the Black-headed Gull *(Larus ridibundus ridibundus L.)* and related species. Behaviour Suppl. IV:1-201.
    1955b. Types of hostile display. Auk 72:247-259.
    1958a. Notes on the behavior of some North American gulls. II: Non-aerial hostile behavior of adults. Behaviour 12:95-182.
    1958b. Notes on the behavior of some North American gulls. III: Pairing behavior. Behaviour 13:112-130.
    1959a. Notes on the behavior of some North American gulls. IV: The ontogeny of hostile behavior and display patterns. Behaviour 14:214-239.
    1959b. A revision of the family Laridae (Aves). Amer. Mus. Novit. 1928:1-42.
    1962. Hostile and sexual behavior patterns of South American and Pacific Laridae. Behaviour Suppl. VIII:1-365.
    1970. Control, suppression, decay, disappearance and replacement of displays. J. Theor. Biol. 29:85-112.

MURPHY, R. C.
    1936. Oceanic birds of South America. New York, Amer. Mus. Nat. Hist.

NELSON, J. B.
    1968a. Breeding behaviour of the Swallow-tailed Gull in the Galápagos. Behaviour 30:146-174.
    1968b. Galapagos: Islands of birds. New York, Morrow.

PARSONS, J.
  1972. Egg size, laying date and incubation period in the Herring Gull. Ibis 114:536-541.
PHILLIPS, G. C.
  1962. Survival value of the white coloration of gulls and other seabirds. D. Phil. thesis, Univ. of Oxford.
PRIESTLEY, C. H. B.
  1957. The heat balance of sheep standing in the sun. Austral. J. Agr. Res. 8:271-280.
RIDGWAY, R.
  1919. The birds of North and Middle America. Pt. VIII. U. S. Nat. Mus. Bull. 50.
ROBERTS, T. S.
  1900. An account of the nesting habits of Franklin's Rosy Gull *(Larus franklinii)*, as observed at Heron Lake in southern Minnesota. Auk 17:272-283.
ROMANOFF, A. L.
  1960. The avian embryo. New York, Macmillan.
SCHLEGER, A. V.
  1962. Physiological attributes of coat colour in beef cattle. Austral. J. Agr. Res. 13:943-959.
SIPLE, P. A.
  1949. Clothing and climate. *In:* Physiology of heat regulation and the science of clothing, ed. L. H. Newburgh. Philadelphia and London, Saunders.
SMITH, J. E., and K. L. DIEM
  1972. Growth and development of young California Gulls *(Larus californicus)*. Condor 74:462-470.
SMITH, W. J.
  1963. Vocal communication of information in birds. Amer. Natur. 97:117-125.
  1965. Message, meaning, and context in ethology. Amer. Natur. 99:405-409.
  1969. Messages of vertebrate communication. Science 165:145-150.
SNOW, B. K. and D. W. SNOW
  1969. Observations on the Lava Gull *Larus fuliginosus*. Ibis 111:30-35.
TINBERGEN, N.
  1953. The Herring Gull's world. London, Collins.
  1959. Comparative studies of the behaviour of gulls (Laridae): A progress report. Behaviour 15:1-70.
  1964. On adaptive radiation in gulls (Tribe Larini). Zool. Mededelingen 39:209-223.
VERMEER, K.
  1963. The breeding ecology of the Glaucous-winged Gull *(Larus glaucescens)* on Mandarte Island, B.C. Occ. Papers Brit. Col. Prov. Mus. 13:1-104.
  1970. Breeding biology of California and Ring-billed Gulls. Can. Wildlife Serv. Rep. Ser. 12, Ottawa.
WILSON, E. O.
  1972. Animal communication. Sci. Amer. 227:52-60.

PLATES

Gray Gulls probing for *Emerita analoga*.

Pursuit flight in the nesting colony. The highest point in the right background is Cerro Colupo.

Pair of Gray Gulls at nest site. The male, at left, is in Oblique Posture.

Rock-standing at midday by nonincubating Gray Gull while mate, in foreground, shades the nest.

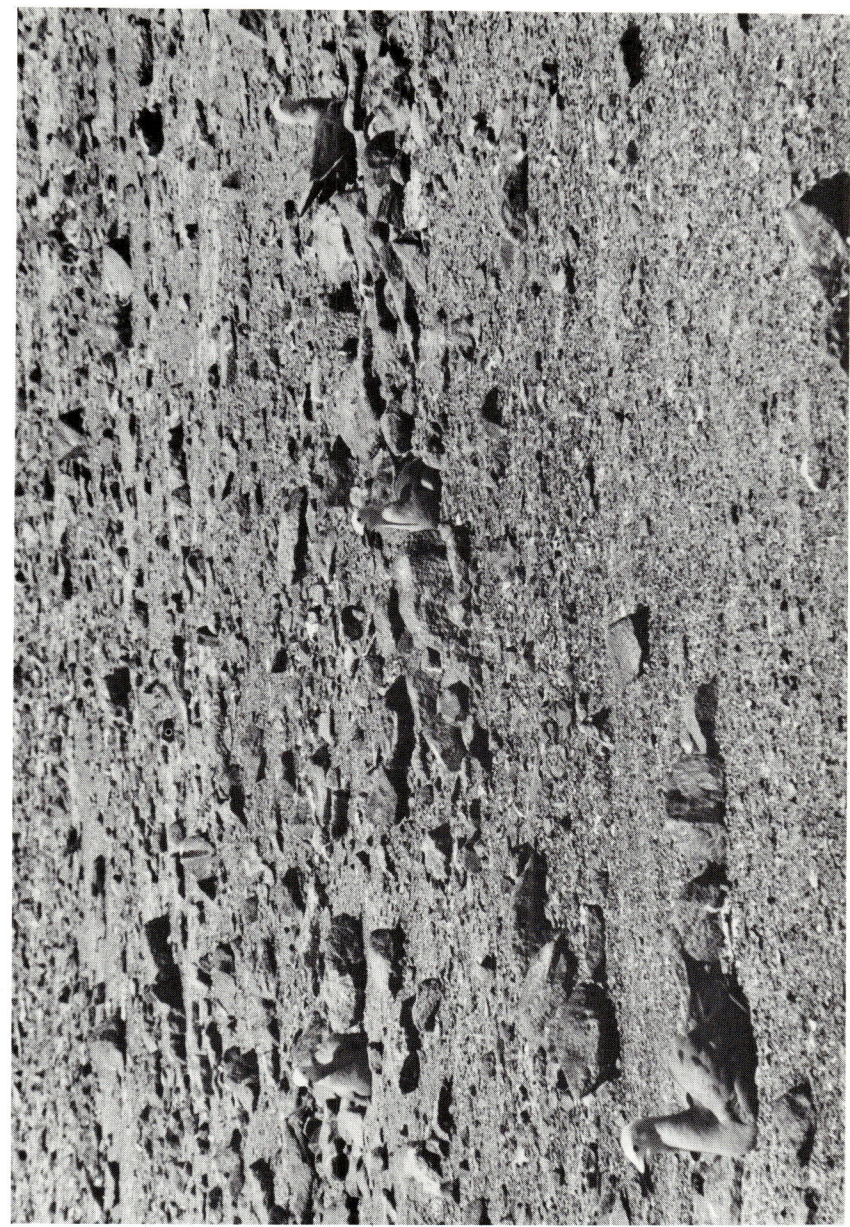

Four incubating Gray Gulls, showing typical nesting habitat and approximate minimum distances between nests.

Nest scrape of Gray Gull with full clutch of two.

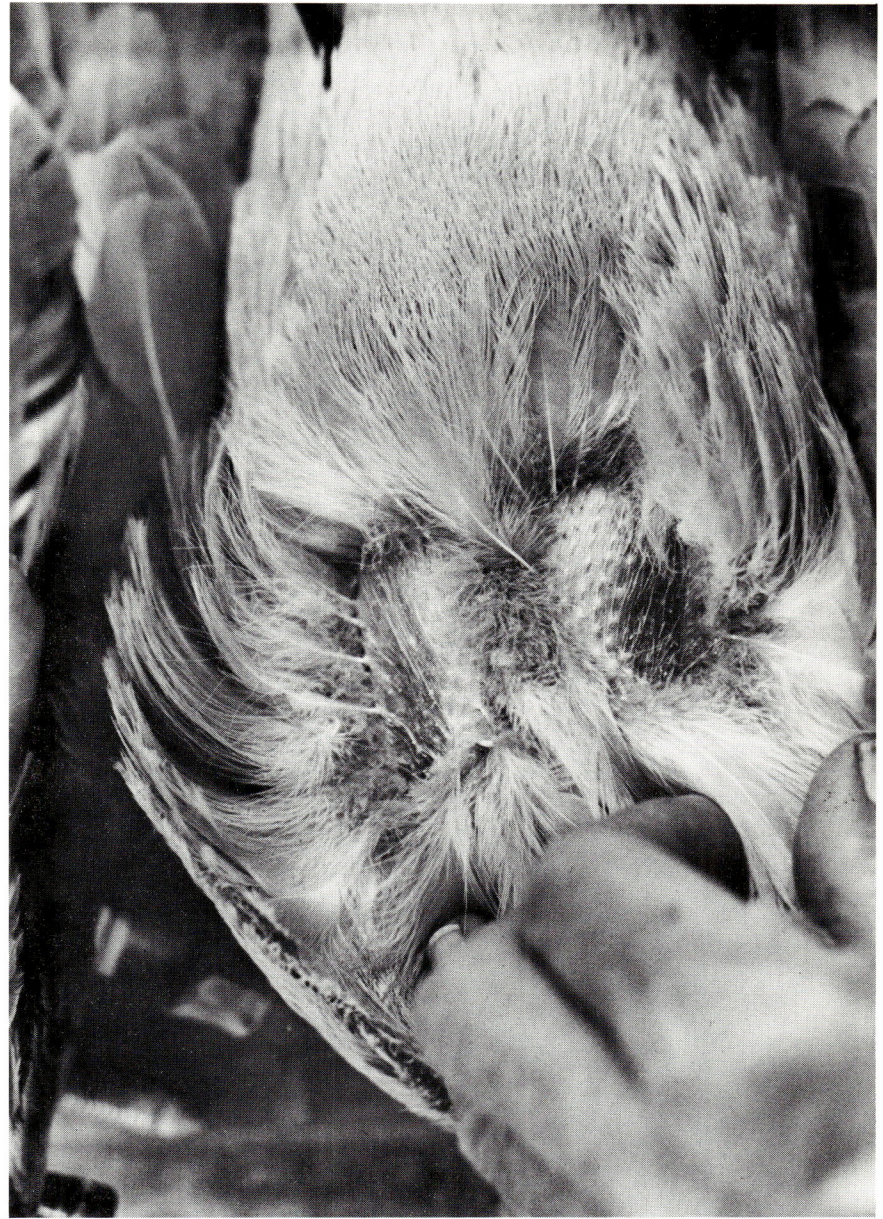

Two-part incubation patch of Gray Gull.

Gray Gull in moderately Hunched Posture approaching its mate to change places on the nest at night; note eye-shine.

Gray Gull shading nest at midday, showing maximal ruffling of feathers.

Incubating Gray Gull panting; back and scapular feathers are partly wind-ruffled.

Newly hatched Gray Gull chick and pipped egg.

Recently hatched Gray Gull chicks showing salt crust around nostrils.

Gray Gull shading chick.

Gray Gull rock-standing with large chicks seeking shade; one chick is yawning.

Adult Gray Gull just after attacking chick; note down feathers on bill. Chick is in Beak-hiding Posture, with head to right.

Adult Gray Gull giving Long Call while shading chicks; note that carpal joints are not abducted. Stake in background marks nest site.

Gray Gull giving Long Call with carpal joints moderately abducted. Note chicks in shade, and adult in background giving Foot-look.

Adult Gray Gull in Low Oblique Posture about to disgorge food for chick.

Choking by two adult Gray Gulls.

Hunched Posture of adult Gray Gull walking to its nest.

Gray Gull chick weighing 226 g, age uncertain.

WITHDRAWN